P9-EDV-073

The Private Prayers of POPE JOHN PAUL II

An Invitation to Prayer

Joannes Paulus PP. II

The Private Prayers of Pope John Paul II

Words of Inspiration

An Invitation to Prayer

The Private Prayers of POPE JOHN PAUL II

An Invitation to Prayer

POCKET BOOKS
New York London Toronto Sydney Singapore

POCKET BOOKS, a division of Simon & Schuster, Inc.
1230 Avenue of the Americas, New York, NY 10020

Original Italian language edition published in Italy in 1999 by
Libreria Editrice Rogate as *Invito Alla Preghiera.*

Published under agreement with Compulsion Sub, LLC,
the exclusive world-wide licensee of the original Italian publication of
The Private Prayers of Pope John Paul II.

ISBN: 0-7434-4439-6

First Pocket Books hardcover printing March 2002

10 9 8 7 6 5 4 3 2 1

For information regarding special discounts for bulk purchases, please
contact Simon & Schuster Special Sales at 1-800-456-6798 or
business@simonandschuster.com

Printed in the U.S.A.

EDITOR'S NOTE

This edition is a translation of the original work *Invito alla Preghiera ("An Invitation to Prayer")* published in Italian in the Vatican City State. Like the previous book in this series, "*Words of Inspiration,*" "*An Invitation to Prayer*" retains the organization of the Vatican original.

CONTENTS

INTRODUCTION

It is difficult to talk about prayer today. People do not pray as much as they used to. In our secularized world the desire and the capacity for prayer have languished, and a special effort will be required to revive it. But for this very reason there is a real need for prayer, *in* the world and *for* the world.

Thus John Paul II becomes the model. He is the teacher of prayer. With his words, but especially by his example, he reminds us that first we must believe, then we must be active, and finally we must pray. He assigns an essential importance to prayer; he affirms the primacy of prayer everywhere.

Prayer is duty
is need,
is comfort,
is hope,
is beauty.

For John Paul II, this is a historic moment for vigorous, forceful prayer.

A profound and gentle prayer, so that men may be reconciled with one another;

a forceful prayer so that justice may prevail;

a humble prayer, so that we may gain the virtue of forgiveness and the return of worthy desires;

a prayer burning with faith, which deserves the aid of the heavenly Father in his omnipotence.

John Paul II makes us understand that his only "politics" consists in words (said with faith and love) and in prayer.

Starting here, then, is the call to prayer! This book offers the wonderful prayers of John Paul II, so that we may learn to restore primacy to prayer, and so our whole existence may live and breathe in prayer.

Prayer

"Totus tuus ego sum
et omnia mea tua sunt.
Accipio te in mea omnia!"

I am entirely yours,
and all that I have is yours.
Be my guide in all things.

The Church exists for prayer

I would like to speak to you about the *call to prayer.*

We have meditated on these words of Jesus: *"Pray that you may have strength... to stand before the Son of man."* And we welcome again today the call to prayer that comes from Christ himself to each of us and to the whole Church. *The call to prayer places the Church's full commitment in the proper perspective.* In 1976, Paul VI, speaking of the "call to commitment," declared that *"in the tradition of the Church every call to action is first of all a call to prayer."* These words have great significance today, too. They are a stimulus for the Church everywhere in the world.

The universal Church of Christ, and hence every particular church, *exists for prayer.* In prayer the individual expresses his nature; the community expresses its vocation; the Church approaches God. In prayer the Church enters into communion with the Father and with his Son, Jesus Christ. *In prayer the Church expresses her Trinitarian life,* because it is directed to the Father, is subjected to the action of the Holy Spirit, and lives fully the relationship with Christ. Indeed, *it is experienced* as the Body of Christ, as mystical Christ.

The Church encounters Christ in prayer in the depths of her being. In this way she discovers the truth of his teachings and assumes his mentality. Seeking to live a personal relationship with Christ, the Church fully realizes the personal dignity of her members. In prayer the Church focuses on Christ; she takes Christ; she takes possession of him, she tastes his friendship, and thus is able to communicate it. Without prayer, all this would be lacking and the Church would have nothing to offer the world. But through the exercise of faith, hope, and charity in prayer, her capacity to communicate Christ is strengthened.

Prayer *is the objective of every catechesis* in the Church, since it is a means of union with God. Through prayer the Church expresses the authority of God and fulfills the first and great commandment of love.

Every aspect of human existence is marked by prayer. *Man's work is revolutionized by prayer,* raised to its highest level. Prayer is the means by which work is fully humanized. In prayer the value of work is understood, because we grasp the fact that we are truly collaborators with God in the action of transforming and elevating the world. Prayer consecrates this collaboration. At the same time prayer is a way of confronting the problems of life, and in prayer every pastoral undertaking is conceived and carried forward.

The call to prayer must precede the call to action, but the call to action must in fact accompany the call to prayer. *The Church finds in prayer the root of social commitment*—the capacity to motivate and sustain it. In prayer we discover the needs of our brothers and sisters and make them our needs, because in prayer we discover that their needs are the needs of Christ. *Social consciousness is formed by prayer.* According to the words of Jesus, justice and mercy are the "weightier matters of the law." The Church's commitment to justice and her search for mercy will be successful only if the Holy Spirit gives the gift of perseverance: this gift must be sought in prayer.

In prayer we arrive at an understanding of the beatitudes and the reasons for living them. Only through prayer can we begin to see the aspirations of men according to the perspective of Christ. Without the intuitions of prayer we would never be able to grasp *all the dimensions of human development* and the urgency, for the Christian community, of commitment to this work.

Prayer invites us to examine our consciences with regard to all the problems that afflict humanity. It invites us to evaluate our responsibilities, personal and collective, before God's judgment and in the light of human solidarity. For this reason, prayer transforms the world. Everything is renewed, both in individuals and in communities. *New goals and new ideals emerge.* Dignity and Christian action are reaffirmed. The promises of baptism, confirmation, and Holy Orders acquire new urgency. Prayer opens up the horizons of conjugal love and of the mission of the family.

Christian sensibility depends on prayer. Prayer is the essential condition—even if not the only one—*for a correct reading of the "signs of the times."* Without prayer we are inevitably deceived on this delicate subject.

Decisions require prayer; major decisions require intense prayer. Jesus himself gave us the example. Before calling together the disciples so that he could choose twelve of them, Jesus spent the night on the mountain, in communion with the Father. For Jesus, praying to the Father did not mean only light and strength. It meant also trust, abandonment, and joy. His human nature exulted in the joy of prayer. In every age, the intensity of the Church's joy is proportionate to her prayer.

The strength of her authority and the condition for her confidence are fidelity to prayer. The mysteries of Christ are revealed to those who approach him in prayer. The full application of the Second Vatican Council will always be conditional on prayer. The great strides made by lay people in the Church in understanding how much they belong to the Church can be explained, in the final analysis, only by grace and its acceptance in prayer.

In the life of the Church today we often notice that *the gift of prayer is joined to the Word of God.* A renewed discovery of the Sacred Scriptures has developed the fruits of prayer. The word of God, accepted and meditated on, has the power to bring our hearts into closer communion with the Holy Trinity. This happens more and more in the Church of today. The benefits we receive through prayer that is joined to the Word of God impel us to respond with more prayer (prayers of praise and thanksgiving).

The Word of God generates prayer in all communities. At the same time it is in prayer that the Word of God is understood, applied, and lived. For all of us who are ministers of the Gospel, with the pastoral responsibility to announce the Good News *opportune et importune*—in season and out of season—and to carefully examine the reality of daily life in the light of the sacred Word of God, prayer is the context in which we prepare the declaration of faith. *All evangelization is prepared for in prayer;* in prayer first of all it applies to ourselves; in prayer it is then offered to the world.

Every local church is truly itself in the degree to which it is a community of prayer, with all the resulting dynamism that prayer effects. The universal Church is never so much herself as when she reflects faithfully the image of Christ in prayer: the Son who, praying, turns his entire being to the Father and consecrates himself for love of his brothers, *"that they also may be consecrated in truth."*

For this reason, dear brothers in the Episcopate, I wish to encourage you in all your efforts *to teach people to pray.* It is the job of the Apostolic Church to transmit the teachings of Jesus to all the generations, to offer faithfully to every local church the response of Jesus to the request: *"Teach us to pray."* I assure you of my support and that of the whole Church in your commitment *to preach the importance of daily prayer and give the example of prayer.* From the words of Jesus we know that wherever two or three are gathered in his name, he is among them. And we know that in every local church gathered in prayer around the bishop lives the incomparable beauty of the entire Catholic Church as the faithful image of Christ in prayer.

In his task as pastor of the universal Church, the successor of Peter is called on to live a communion of prayer with his brother bishops and their dioceses, and for this reason all your initiatives to promote prayer have my full support. In fraternal and pastoral charity I am near you when you call your people to daily prayer, when you invite them to discover in prayer their dignity as Christians. *Every diocesan or parish initiative* that exhorts us to more intense prayer, on the part of both individuals and families, is a blessing for the universal Church. Every group that gathers to recite the Rosary is a gift for the Kingdom of God. Yes, wherever two or three are gathered in the name of Christ, he is there. The contemplative communities are a special gift of God's love for his people. They need and deserve the fullness of your love and pastoral support. Their particular job in the world is to testify to the supremacy of God and the primacy of Christ's love, *"which surpasses all understanding."*

Profoundly convinced of the power of prayer and humbly engaged in it, dear brothers, we confidently proclaim throughout the whole Church the call to prayer. At stake is the very necessity for the Church to be herself, the Church at prayer, for the glory of the Father. The Holy Spirit will assist us and the merits of the Paschal Mystery of Christ will make up for our human weakness.

The example of Mary, the Mother of Jesus, as the model of prayer, is a source of confident trust for all of us. Looking at her, we are aware that her example sustains our priests, religious, and lay people. We know that her generosity is an inheritance for the whole Church to proclaim and imitate.

TO A GROUP OF AMERICAN BISHOPS
ON A VISIT *"AD LIMINA"**
JUNE 10, 1988

* The visit *ad limina* means, technically, the obligation incumbent on the bishops of visiting, at stated times, the "thresholds of the Apostles," Sts. Peter and Paul, and of presenting themselves before the Pope to give an account of the state of their dioceses.

Prayer, the breath of Christian life

"Stay with us, for it is getting toward evening."

This is the invocation that rises spontaneously from the soul who is before Christ, present at the Sacrament of the Eucharist.

At the start of my Papacy I said that for me prayer is the first task and, as it were, the first proclamation, just as it is the first condition of my service in the Church and in the world. I here reaffirm that every person consecrated to the priestly ministry or the religious life, and, indeed, every believer, must always consider prayer the essential and irreplaceable work of his vocation, the *opus divinum,* the divine work, that precedes—at the core, as it were, of life and work—any other undertaking. We well know that faithfulness to prayer or its abandonment is the test of the vitality or the decadence of the religious life, of the Apostolate, of Christian faith.

Those who have felt the joy of praying know that there is something ineffable about the experience, and that the only way to understand the depths of its richness is to live it: one learns what prayer is by praying. In words, one merely attempts to stammer out something: praying means to enter into the mystery of communion with God, who reveals himself to the soul in all the wealth of his infinite love; it means to enter into the heart of Jesus, to know his feelings. Praying also means to anticipate on this earth the mystery of the transfiguring contemplation of God, who will make himself visible outside of time, in eternity.

Thus prayer is a theme infinite in its substance, and infinite as well in our experience, since the gift of prayer is multiplied in those who pray, according to the manifold, unparalleled, and astounding wealth of divine grace that comes to us as we pray.

In prayer is the Spirit of God that leads us to knowledge of our deepest inner truth and reveals to us that we belong to the body of Christ, which is the Church. And the Church is aware that one of her fundamental tasks is to communicate to the world the experience of prayer: to the simple man as to the intellectual, to the contemplative man as to the one who is overburdened by activity.

The Church embodies in prayer her vocation as the guide of every human being who, before the mystery of God, finds that he is in need of enlightenment and support, discovering that he is poor and humble, but also sincerely attracted by the desire to encounter God and speak to him.

Jesus is our prayer. This should be the first thought of faith when we want to pray. By becoming man, the Word of God assumed our humanity in order to bring it to God the Father as a new creation, capable of talking to him, contemplating him, experiencing with him a supernatural communion of life through grace.

The union with the Father, which Jesus reveals in his prayer, is a sign for us. Jesus joins us to his prayer, he is the fundamental model and source of the gift of worship, in which he, as the head, involves the whole Church.

Jesus carries on in us the gift of his prayer, asking us, as it were, for the loan of our minds, our hearts, and our lips, so that as long as men exist on the earth so will prayer, which began in his Incarnation and which he continues forever, in his very humanity, in Heaven.

We know, however, that in our earthly situation there is always some work to do in order to pray well, some obstacle to overcome. Spontaneously, the question arises about the circumstances of prayer. In that regard the classic works of spirituality offer some useful suggestions that take account of the realities of our human condition. First of all, prayer requires *the exercise of the presence of God,* as the spiritual masters called that profound act of faith which makes us aware that when we pray God is with us, he inspires us and listens to us, takes our words seriously. Without this preceding act of faith our prayer might remain more easily distracted from its principal end, that of being a moment of true dialogue with the Lord.

In order to pray, furthermore, we must create in ourselves a profound inner silence. Prayer is true if at prayer we do not seek ourselves but only the Lord. We must immerse ourselves in the will of God with a naked spirit, open to total dedication to God. We will then realize that every prayer of ours, by its nature, converges on the prayer that Jesus taught us and that became his only prayer on Gethsemane: *"Not my will but thine be done."*

Finally, we must keep in mind that in prayer we are, with Jesus, *ambassadors from the world to the Father.* All humanity needs to find in prayer its own voice: for humanity is in need of redemption, of forgiveness, of purification. What weighs on us must also enter into our prayer, along with what we are ashamed of; that which by its nature separates us from God, but which belongs to our frailty or to the poverty of our individual persons. Thus Peter prayed after the miracle of the fish, saying to Jesus: *"Depart from me, for I am a sinful man, O Lord."*

This prayer, which originates in the humility of our experience of sin, and which is allied with our moral poverty, touches the merciful heart of God; those who pray become newly aware of the attitude of the prodigal son, who moved the Father's heart.

Praying is not an imposition; it is a gift. It is not a constriction, it is a possibility; it is not a weight, it is a joy. But to taste this joy we must create the proper disposition in our spirit.

For this reason, we find on our lips the invocation of the Apostles:

> *"Lord, teach us to pray."*
> Yes, Lord Jesus,
> train us in this special knowledge,
> the only one necessary,
> the only one within reach of all,
> the only one that will cross the bounds of time
> to follow you into the house of your Father,
> when we, too, *"shall be like him,*
> *for we shall see him as he is."*
> Teach us, Lord,
> this divine science; that is enough for us.

November 24, 1984

Lord, teach us to pray!

Lord, teach us to pray!

When the Apostles, on the slopes of the Mount of Olives, addressed these words to Jesus, they weren't just asking an ordinary question but expressing with spontaneous trust one of the deepest needs of the human heart.

In truth, the modern world does not make much room for that need. The frenetic rhythm of daily activities, along with the noisy and often frivolous invasions of telephones, faxes, and other kinds of communications, does not, certainly, constitute a favorable climate for the inner concentration required by prayer. There are further, more profound difficulties: in modern man the religious view of the world and of life has become more and more attenuated. The process of secularization seems to have persuaded him that the course of events has sufficient explanation in the play of forces present in this world, independent of higher interventions. In addition, the achievements of science and technology have fostered in him the conviction that he can already in great measure today, and still more tomorrow, control situations, shaping them according to his own desires.

Thus even in Christian environments a "functional" view of prayer has become widespread, a view that risks compromising prayer's transcendent character. The true encounter with God, some affirm, is realized in opening up to one's neighbor. Thus prayer should not be a removal of oneself from the dissipation of the world to recollect oneself in dialogue with God; rather, it should be expressed in the unconditional commitment to charity toward others. True prayer would therefore be works of charity, and those alone.

In reality, the human being, who, as a creation, is in himself incomplete and needy, turns spontaneously to him who is the source of every gift, to praise him, petition him, and seek in him the satisfaction of the powerful yearning that burns in his heart. Clearly St. Augustine understood this when he wrote: *"You have made us for you, O Lord, and our heart has no peace until it rests in you."*

For this very reason, the experience of prayer, as a fundamental act of the believer, is common to all religions, even those in which faith in a personal God is vague or is obscured by false representations.

Prayer belongs in particular to the Christian religion, in which it occupies a central place. Jesus exhorts us to *"always pray, and not lose heart."* The Christian knows that prayer is as necessary to him as breath and, having once tasted the sweetness of intimate conversation with God, does not hesitate to immerse himself in it with trusting abandon.

GENERAL AUDIENCE,
SEPTEMBER 9, 1992

Christian prayer has its roots in the Old Testament

Christian prayer has its roots in the Old Testament. It is, in fact, intimately bound up in the religious experience of the people of Israel, for whom God wanted to reserve the revelation of his mystery.

Unlike pagan populations, pious Israelites know "the face" of God and can turn to him with trust in the name of the Covenant stipulated at the foot of Mount Sinai. Yahweh is prayed to in Israel as the creator of the universe, the master of human destiny, the worker of the most extraordinary miracles, but he is above all the God *of the Covenant.* That knowledge is the basis of the trust with which he is invoked in every circumstance.

Trust, but also *profound veneration and respect.* In fact, it was God who initiated the Covenant. Thus, the basic attitude of one praying to him is that of the *listener.* Doesn't the Shema, the daily profession of faith with which the Israelite starts every day, begin with this exhortation: "Hear, O Israel: The LORD our God is one LORD."

Not by chance does the *adoration of the one God* constitute the first commandment of the law, from which flows, as from its highest source, every other moral duty. The pact of the Covenant with the "just" and "Holy" God can't help committing the believer to conduct worthy of such an exalted Interlocutor. No prayer could fill the needs of an improper moral life. Jesus will one day remind the Pharisees, in a particularly meaningful text of Hosea: *"For I desire steadfast love and not sacrifice, the knowledge of God, rather than burnt offerings."*

As an *encounter with the God of the Covenant,* the prayer of the faithful Jew is not, as for pagans, a monologue addressed to deaf and mute idols but a true dialogue with a God who in the past has revealed himself many times, in words and deeds, and who even in the present continues to make his saving presence felt in various ways.

Furthermore, it is a prayer whose connotations are predominantly communal: the individual feels able to speak to God precisely because he belongs to the people chosen by him. Yet the *individual* dimension is there as well: one need only leaf through the "handbook" of Biblical prayer, the Book of Psalms, to hear the eloquent echoes of the personal piety of the individual Israelite.

The prophets, too, insistently compel us to that piety. In the face of the recurring temptations of outward form and empty show, as in situations of discouragement and distrust, the work of the prophets is constantly directed at recalling the Israelites to a *more inner and spiritual* devotion, from which alone can spring a true experience of communion with Yahweh.

Thus, even as Old Testament prayer reaches its height, it is preparing its definitive form, which it will assume with the Incarnation of the Word of God.

GENERAL AUDIENCE,
SEPTEMBER 16, 1992

With the Incarnation of the Word of God the history of prayer takes a decisive turn

With the Incarnation of the Word of God the *history of prayer* takes a *decisive turn.* In Jesus, Heaven and earth meet, God is reconciled with humanity, the dialogue between the creation and its Creator is renewed. Jesus is the *definitive offering* of the love of the Father and at the same time the *full and irrevocable response* of man to divine expectations. He, the Word Incarnate, is therefore the unique Mediator, offering to God the Father every sincere prayer that comes from the human heart.

The demand that the first Disciples addressed to Jesus then becomes our demand, too: *"Lord, teach us to pray."*

As Jesus taught them, so also he "teaches" us. He does it above all by example. How can one not recall the touching prayer with which he addresses the Father in the first moment of the Incarnation?

After that, there is no important moment in the life of Christ that is not accompanied by prayer. At the beginning of his public mission, the Holy Spirit descends upon him *"when Jesus also had been baptized and was praying."* From the Gospel of Mark we know that, *just as he was about to preach in Galilee, Jesus, "in the morning, a great while before day, rose and went out to a lonely place, and there he prayed."* Before choosing the Apostles *"he went out to the mountain to pray; and all night he continued in prayer."* Before promising Peter primacy, Jesus, according to Luke, "was praying alone." Also at the moment of the Transfiguration, when, before the shadows thickened to darkness on Calvary, his glory shone forth, Jesus prayed.

Especially revealing is the prayer in which, during the Last Supper, Jesus pours forth to the Father his feelings of love, praise, supplication, trusting abandon. These are the same feelings that reemerge in the garden of Gethsemane and on the Cross, from which he offers us the example of that last, moving invocation: *"Father, forgive them, for they know not what they do."*

Jesus teaches us to pray *with his words* as well. To underline that *"they ought always to pray and not lose heart,"* he tells the parable of the evil judge and the widow. Later he counsels: *"Watch and pray that you may not enter into temptation; the spirit indeed is willing, but the flesh is weak."* And he insists: *"Ask, and it will be given you; seek, and you will find; knock, and it will be opened to you. For every one who asks receives, and he who seeks finds, and to him who knocks it will be opened."*

Jesus then teaches the Disciples, eager for a practical guide, the sublime formula of the Our Father, which will become through the centuries the typical prayer of the Christian community. Tertullian described it as a *brevarium totius evangelii,* "a compendium of the entire Gospel." In it Jesus delivers the essence of his message. Those who recite the Our Father with awareness "implicate themselves" in the Gospel: they must accept the consequences for their own lives that come from the evangelical message, of which the Lord's Prayer is the most authentic expression.

GENERAL AUDIENCE,
SEPTEMBER 23, 1992

Why pray?

We must "always pray and not lose heart."

Why must we pray?

We must pray first of all because we are believers.

Prayer is in fact the recognition of our limits and our dependence: we come from God, we are of God, and to God we return! We can therefore only abandon ourselves to him, our Lord and Creator, with absolute, total trust.

Prayer is first of all an act of intelligence, a feeling of humility and gratefulness, an attitude of trust and abandonment to the one who gave us his life for love.

Prayer is a mysterious but real dialogue with God, a dialogue of confidence and love.

We are, however, Christians, and so we must pray as Christians.

In fact, for the Christian prayer acquires a special character, which changes its intimate nature and its intimate value.

The Christian is a disciple of Jesus; he believes truly that Jesus is the Word Incarnate; the Son of God come among us on this earth.

Therefore, the Christian knows that his prayer is Jesus; every one of his prayers starts from Jesus; it is he who prays in us, with us, for us.

All those who believe in God pray; but the Christian prays in Jesus Christ: Christ is our prayer!

The greatest prayer is the Holy Mass, because in the Holy Mass Jesus himself is fully present, as he renews the sacrifice of the Cross; but every prayer is valid, especially the Our

Father, which he himself wished to teach the Apostles and all men on earth.

Saying the words of the Our Father, Jesus created a specific and, at the same time, universal model. Indeed, all that we can and must say to the Father is contained in those seven requests, which we all know by heart. They are so simple that even a child can learn them, but at the same time so profound that one can spend a lifetime meditating on their meaning.

Finally, we must continue to pray because we are frail and full of guilt.

We must recognize humbly and realistically that we are poor creatures, confused in our ideas, tempted to evil, frail and weak, continually in need of inner strength and comfort.

- —Prayer gives us the strength for grand ideals, the strength to maintain our faith, charity, purity, generosity;
- —Prayer gives us the courage to emerge from indifference and sin if, unfortunately, we have yielded to temptation and weakness;
- —Prayer gives us light by which to see and to consider the events of our own life and of history itself in the salvific perspective of God and eternity.

Therefore, do not stop praying! Do not let a day pass without praying a little! Prayer is a duty, but it is also a great joy, because it is a dialogue with God through Jesus Christ.

Celebrate the Holy Mass every Sunday, and if possible sometimes during the week as well; every day say prayers in the morning and evening and at any other opportune moments!

MARCH 14, 1979

The Holy Spirit at the origin of prayer

The primary and highest form of inner life is prayer. The doctors and spiritual masters are so convinced of it that often they present the inner life as the life of prayer. The principal author of this life is the Holy Spirit, as he was in Christ.

We know that during his messianic activities the Teacher often withdrew into solitude to pray, and that he spent entire nights in prayer. For this he preferred solitary places, which lend themselves to conversation with God, responding to the need and inclination of the soul that is sensitive to the mystery of divine transcendence. Analogously, so did Moses and Elijah, as the Old Testament tells us. The Book of the Prophet Hosea demonstrates that *in solitary places there is a special inspiration to prayer;* God, in fact, *"leads us into the wilderness to speak to the heart."*

In our life, too, as in that of Jesus, the Holy Spirit turns out to be the Spirit of prayer. In a way, therefore, *the Holy Spirit transmits into our hearts the prayer of the Son*, who addresses that cry to the Father. So, too, our prayer expresses our *"adoption as sons,"* which is granted in Christ and through Christ. Prayer professes our faith, conscious of the truth that *"we are children"* and *"heirs of God," "fellow heirs with Christ."* Prayer allows us to live this supernatural reality thanks to the action of the Holy Spirit that *"bears witness with our spirit."*

In reality, especially in the teaching of St. Paul, the Holy Spirit appears as the author of Christian prayer, above all because he spurs us to prayer. It is he who generates the need and the desire to *"watch and pray,"* as Christ recommends, especially in the hour of temptation, because *"the spirit indeed is willing, but the flesh is weak."*

With great penetration, in the letter to the Romans, the Apostle shows how *"the Spirit helps us in our weakness; for we do not know how to pray as we ought, but the Spirit himself intercedes for us with sighs too deep for words."*

We are at the inmost and deepest root of prayer. Paul points out and then makes us understand that the Holy Spirit *not only spurs us to prayer* but *prays in us himself!*

The Holy Spirit is at the source of the prayer that most perfectly reflects the relationship existing between the divine Persons of the Trinity: the prayer of *glorification* and *thanksgiving*, with which the Father is honored, and with him the Son and the Holy Spirit.

The glorification of the One and Triune God, through the action of the Holy Spirit who prays in us and through us occurs principally in our hearts, but is translated also into *spoken praise*, because of the need for personal expression and communal coming together in celebrating the marvels of God. The soul that loves God expresses itself in words and readily, too, in song, as has always been the case in the Church, ever since the early Christian communities. Music can be helpful in praising God, when the instruments serve to "transport on high"—*rapere in celsitudinem*—"human affections" (St. Thomas Aquinas). That is the explanation of the value of singing and music in the Liturgy of the Church, as "they serve to excite affection toward God . . . [also] with different modulations of sounds" (St. Thomas). All this happens when both individual souls and the community encourage the inner action of the Holy Spirit.

GENERAL AUDIENCE,
APRIL 17, 1991

Family prayer

The family has always been at the center of ecclesial attention.

If we ask the "why" of such interest, it is not difficult to find it in the *love and service that the Church owes man.* Christianity is the religion of the Incarnation, it is the joyous proclamation of a God who comes to meet man and becomes man.

For this reason, ever since my first encyclical, I have not hesitated to affirm that man is the *"Way of the Church,"* intending by that to recall and as it were retrace the road traversed by God himself, when, through the Incarnation and the Redemption, he set off on the path of his creation.

But how to meet man, without meeting the family? Man is essentially a "social" being; more accurately, one could say a *"family"* being. The family is the natural place of his coming into the world, it is the environment in which normally he receives what he needs in order to develop, it is the primordial emotional nucleus that gives him coherence and confidence, it is the first school of social relations.

We can say: here is "the Gospel of the family," which the Church intends to present with renewed energy. This year, which the Lord offers to us, will be testimony and proclamation, a time of reflection and a time of conversion: *a time of special prayer,* prayer *for* families, prayer *in* families, prayer *of* families.

It is time to discover the value of prayer, its mysterious force, its capacity not only to lead us back to God but to introduce us to the *radical truth of the human being.*

When a person prays, he places himself before God, a you, a divine you, and at the same time grasps the inmost truth of his own "I": You the divine, I the human, the personal being created in the image of God.

This occurs similarly in *family prayer:* placing itself in the light of the Lord, the family feels that it is profoundly a *communal subject,* a "we" cemented by an eternal design of love, that nothing in the world can destroy.

We look at Mary, the Bride and the Mother of the Family of Nazareth. She is a living icon of prayer, *in a family of prayer.* Precisely for this reason she is also the image of serenity and peace, of giving and faith, of tenderness and hope. And what she is, every family must be, too.

> Holy Virgin, we ask you
> to teach us to pray.
> We ask of you
> the great gift of love
> in all the families of the world.

ANGELUS,
JANUARY 30, 1994

How can the family of today transmit the faith?

There are two things that Catholic families can do immediately to strengthen family life. *The first is to pray:* both individual and family prayer. Prayer raises our minds and hearts to God to thank him for his blessings, to ask him for help. And that introduces the saving power of Jesus Christ into the decisions and activities of daily life.

There is one prayer in particular that I recommend for families: *the Rosary.* And especially the Joyful Mysteries, which help us meditate on the Sacred Family of Nazareth. Joining her will to the will of God, Mary conceived the Christ Child, and became the model for every mother who carries a child in her womb. Visiting her cousin Elizabeth, Mary brought to another family the saving presence of Jesus. Mary gave birth to the Baby Jesus in the most humble circumstances and presented him to Simeon in the temple, as every child can be presented to God in baptism. Mary and Joseph worried about the child who was lost before they found him in the temple, just as parents throughout the generations know that the trials and sorrows of family life are the way to a closer union with Jesus. To use a phrase made famous by the late Father Patrick Peyton: *The family that prays together stays together!*

OCTOBER 7, 1995

Prayer of contemplation

Since the Christian inspiration in our culture presupposes recognition of the just and specific realities of the Kingdom of God, the contribution of those who, in prayer and contemplation, derive light from the divine source, to shed it on the entire community, is fundamental. Yes, dear brothers and sisters, let us say it aloud, with true conviction in our hearts: *there is no renewal,* even social, *that does not begin in contemplation.* The encounter with God in prayer introduces into the folds of history a mysterious power that touches hearts, leading them to conversion and renewal, and becoming a potent historical force for the transformation of social structures. Thus in this new season of commitment of the Church the contemplative must feel that they are on the front line, and, following in their footsteps, every believer must seek to make more room in his life for prayer.

FOR THE THIRD CONFERENCE OF THE CHURCH IN ITALY, NOVEMBER 23, 1995

Cultivate both personal and communal prayer

It is appropriate to emphasize here the relevance that prayer has always had in the thinking of Padre Pio. From him you have inherited the conviction that the first, indispensable method for spreading the Kingdom of God among souls is *prayer.* Be worthy guardians of that inheritance! Be so in a special way in these years when we are preparing for the Great Jubilee of 2000.

Cultivate both *personal* prayer, nourished by the Word of God, and *communal* prayer, and always in harmony with the "praying breath" of the Church, which is expressed in the Liturgy. As for Padre Pio, so, too, for you the two hinges of spiritual life are the Sacraments of the Eucharist and of Repentance: Mass and Confession are the preferential means of Paschal dynamism, which originates in the power of Christ.

To the Padre Pio Prayer Groups,
October 5, 1996

The importance of prayer

It is important that intimate conversation with the heavenly Father never be absent from our daily existence. Everything gains meaning and value from this communion of life, so that our lives and our actions may manifest the merciful love of God, the source of unity and communion. If this is valid for every baptized person, it is even more essential for those who are called by Providence to be the luminous reflection of the divine fatherhood before the Christian people entrusted to their apostolic care.

This movement was inspired totally by love: the love that God has for us and that we are called on to reciprocate; love for our brothers and sisters, so that we may make them feel the concern in Christ's heart. This yearning for divine charity becomes the fulcrum of effective action on the part of believers who wish to build a single human family. It becomes, in addition, service to the poor and the needy.

TO THE BISHOPS, FRIENDS OF THE FOCOLARE MOVEMENT, FEBRUARY 12, 1999

A great prayer for the Italian people at the approach of the year 2000

Dear brothers in the Episcopate, our common concern for Italy *cannot be expressed in words alone.* If Italian society is to profoundly renew itself, cleansing itself of suspicion and looking with confidence toward the future, then it is necessary for *all believers to mobilize in communal prayer.* I know through personal experience what such prayer meant in the history of my nation. *With the approach of the year 2000, the entire Church,* and especially in Europe, *needs a great prayer,* that will pass, like successive waves, through the various churches, nations, continents. In this great prayer there is a special place for Italy: and the experience of recent years provides a specific reminder of the need for such prayer. Prayer always means a kind of "confession," a recognition of the presence of God in history and of his work for individuals and nations; at the same time, prayer promotes a closer union with him and encourages individuals to come together.

As bishops of the churches in Italy we must hasten to announce this great prayer for the Italian people, in view of the approach of the year 2000, and in regard to the current situation, in which there is an urgent need to mobilize the spiritual and moral forces of the entire society. It is my conviction, shared also by distinguished Italians who are not practicing Catholics, like the late lamented President Pertini,* that the Church in Italy can do much more than is generally believed. It is a great

* Sandro Pertini, 1896–1990.

social force that unites the inhabitants of Italy, from the north to the south. It is a force that has stood the test of history.

The Church is such a force above all through prayer and the unifying power of prayer. The moment has arrived when this conviction can and must be made concretely real. The very exhortation to such a prayer, the plans for its preparation, its profound motivation in this historical moment are a call to all Italians to reflect and understand. Perhaps they may be an example and a stimulus for other nations.

"Apart from me you can do nothing." The words of Jesus contain the most convincing call to prayer and at the same time the strongest reason for trust in the presence of the Savior among us. This presence is an inexhaustible source of hope and courage even in the bewildering and painful circumstances of the history of individuals and peoples.

JANUARY 6, 1994

The great prayer for Italy: Let us see the signs of your presence

O God, our Father,
we praise you and thank you.
You who love every man
and guide all peoples,
accompany
the steps of our nation,
which are often difficult
but are full of hope.
Let us see
the signs of your presence
and feel
the force of your love
that never fails.
Lord Jesus, Son of God
and Savior of the world,
made man
in the womb of the Virgin Mary,
we confess to you our faith.
May your Gospel
be light and strength
for our personal choices and
those of society.
May your law of love
lead our civil community
to justice and solidarity,
to reconciliation and peace.

Holy Spirit, love
of the Father and of the Son,
confidently we invoke you.
You who are the inner teacher
reveal to us
the thoughts and ways of God.
Grant that we may look
at human events
with pure and penetrating eyes,
that we may preserve the just
    inheritance
of sanctity and civility
of our people,
that we may turn
our hearts and minds
to the renewal of our society.
Glory to you, O Son,
who for love
became our servant.
Glory to you, O Holy Spirit,
who live and reign
to the end of time.
Amen.

MARCH 19, 1994

To God

Openness to Christ . . .
can be achieved
only through an ever more mature
reference to the Father and his love.

Dives in Misericordia
(Encyclical,
November 30, 1980)

To God the Creator

God, you are our Creator.
You are good
and your mercy is infinite.
God, you have given to us men
an inner law
that we must live by.
To do your will
and accomplish our task.
To follow your paths
and know peace in our soul.
To you we offer our obedience.
Guide us in all the initiatives
that we undertake on earth.
Free us from our evil tendencies,
which turn our hearts away
from your will.
Do not allow
us to invoke your name
to justify human strife.
O God, you are the one and only.
You we adore.
Do not let us distance ourselves
  from you.
God, judge of all men,
help us to be among the chosen
on the last day.
God, author of justice and peace,

grant us true joy,
and genuine love,
and enduring brotherhood
among peoples.
Fill us with your eternal gifts.
Amen!

AUGUST 19, 1985

O God, preserve and bless the work that you have done through the centuries

Be gracious, Almighty Father, to these your children, whom you have led from the shadows into the shining light of your truth. Pour into their hearts your Holy Spirit, the Spirit of Truth and the Consoler.

Give piety and wisdom to the shepherds of your people, so that they may lead the flock to the pastures of life. Let them, O Almighty God, exercise their sacred ministry with freedom and serenity.

Spread your light and your strength in the hearts of those whom you have called to consecrate themselves to you, so that they may be persevering and can give themselves without reserve. Multiply the number of those receiving vocations to the priesthood and the religious life, reinforce their generous purpose, and allow them to walk without obstacles on the path of your divine service.

Turn your gaze, O Lord, upon families who live united in your love. May they welcome the gift of life with joy and a sense of responsibility. May they, with your grace, grow in mutual love. May parents be able to offer their children the gift of faith, together with the concrete testimony of an authentically Christian life.

Turn your loving gaze, O God, upon young people. They carry in their hearts a great hope: make them strong and pure, so that they can build their tomorrow with confidence. Let them receive freely the gift of the faith of their fathers, accept it with gratitude, and develop it with generosity.

You are the Lord of peoples and the Father of humanity. I invoke your blessing on this your family: let it heed, in accordance with its conscience, the voice of your call. Membership in your Kingdom of holiness and life should not be judged to be in conflict with the good of our homeland. Let us always and everywhere render you the praise that is due, and bear witness freely and serenely to truth, justice, and charity.

Lord, bless this nation, smile upon it, and give it your peace!

And now, in a spirit of entrustment, I turn to you, sweetest Mother of Christ and our Mother, uniting my voice and that of your children who pray to you, trusting in your intercession. Mother of Mercy, the people flock to you, placing themselves under your protection: do not reject their entreaties in a time of need, preserve them from danger, lead them to your Son.

You, O Mother, are the memory of the Church. You guard in your heart the actions of men and of peoples. I ask you to help them to be now and forever faithful to Christ and the Church.

JUNE 5, 1987

"Though he was rich, he became poor"

We give thanks to you, O Our Father, for the Word that became flesh and, on that night in Bethlehem, came to live among us.

We thank you for the Word, with which you communicate for eternity the holy reality of your divinity.

We thank you for the Word, in which before the beginning of time you decided to create the world, so that it might bear witness to you.

We thank you, because in your Word *you loved man* "before the foundation of the world."

We thank you, because in him, your chosen Son, you decided to *renew all creation;* you decided to *redeem man.*

We thank you, eternal Father, for the night in Bethlehem when God was born, when the Word became flesh and the *power of Redemption* came to live among us.

We thank you for the *inheritance of your grace,* which you have not taken from the heart of man but have renewed through the earthly birth of your Son, so that we, by means of his Cross and his Resurrection, could regain, from generation to generation, the *dignity of children of God,* which was lost through sin, the dignity of adopted brothers of your eternal Son. We give thanks to you, O Holy Father, for your *holy name,* which you have allowed to flower in our hearts through the Redemption of the world.

We thank you, eternal Father, for the *motherhood of the Virgin Mary,* who under the protection of Joseph, the carpenter of Nazareth, brought your Son into the world, in poverty.

We thank you, Heavenly Father, for the Child laid in a manger: in him "the goodness and loving kindness of God our Savior appeared."

We thank you, eternal Father, *for this love,* which comes *like a feeble infant into the story of each man.*

We thank you, because, "though he was rich, he became poor for us, so that we might become rich by means of his poverty."

We thank you for the marvelous *economy of the Redemption* of man and the world, which was revealed for the first time on the night of the birth in Bethlehem.

Our Father!

Look with the eyes of the newborn Child at men who are dying of hunger, while huge sums are committed to weapons. Look at the unspeakable grief of parents who must witness the agony of their children who beg them for bread that they do not have, and that could be procured with even a tiny fraction of the lavish amounts being spent on sophisticated means of destruction, because of which, the clouds that gather on the horizon of humanity become more and more threatening.

Hear, O Father, the cry for peace that rises from populations martyred by war, and speak to the hearts of those who can help to find, through negotiations and dialogue, fair and honorable solutions to the ongoing conflicts.

Look at the anxious and tormented road of so many people who are struggling to find the means of survival, to advance and raise themselves.

Look at the pain and anguish that lacerate the souls of those who are forced to live far from their families or who live in families torn apart by selfishness and infidelity; of those who are without work, without a home, without a country, without love, without hope.

Look at the peoples who are without joy and security, because they see their fundamental rights violated; look at our world of today, with its hopes and its disappointments, with its courage and its cowardice, with its noble ideals and its humiliating compromises.

Urge individuals and peoples to break down the wall of selfishness, of aggression and hatred, to open themselves to fraternal respect toward every individual, near and far, because we are all human, because we are brothers and sisters in Christ.

Enable each of us to bring the necessary aid to those who are in need, to give ourselves for the good of all, to renew our hearts in the grace of Christ the Redeemer.

Help your Church to do its utmost for the poor, for the dispossessed, for the suffering.

Preserve and strengthen in all hearts the yearning for faith in you and kindness toward our brothers; the search for your presence and your love; trust in your redeeming power, confidence in your forgiveness, and abandonment to your Providence.

Jesus Christ, the Son of the living God, born that night in Bethlehem to the Virgin Mary! Jesus Christ, our brother and our Redeemer! With your first look, embrace the troubles that assail the world of today! Born on the earth, receive into your communion all the peoples and nations of the earth.

Receive us all, men and women, your brothers and sisters who are in need of your love and your mercy.

December 25, 1983

Deliver us, O Father

Deliver us, O Father
from the evil that our actions generate
in so many ways when they are reckless.
Make our work
useful to the family of man,
in accordance with your will!
Let it respond to the needs
of this ever-increasing family,
and to the needs of nations and of all
societies.
Make our work
serve to give every individual person
a life worthy of humanity
in justice and peace!

MAY 15, 1985

We entrust the new year to God

To You, who are the beginning without beginning,
the only God,
to you, Father, Son, and Holy Ghost,
to you, who are truth and love,
omnipotence and mercy,
we entrust today this new beginning of human time.
Be present in it and active so that in you "we live and
move and have our being."

Let us unite this first day of the new year with the earthly mystery of the birth of the Word, of the Son whom you, O Father, gave to mankind, so that he might be one of us.

Today, with deep veneration and tender affection, we embrace the Maternity of the Virgin of Nazareth, whom you, O eternal Father, chose to be the Mother of your Son, through the action of the Holy Spirit, who is your love in the mystery of the inscrutable Trinity.

We greet you, O new year, who starting today inscribe yourself in the history of all mankind and, at the same time, in the inner history of each of us.

ANGELUS, JANUARY 1, 1986

For the sick and dying

Almighty and eternal God, Father of the poor, comfort of the sick, hope of the dying, your love guides each moment of our life. We lift our hearts and minds in prayer to you. We glorify you for the gift of human life and especially for the promise of eternal life. We know that you are always near the afflicted and the poor and those who are defenseless and those who suffer.

O God of tenderness and compassion, accept the prayers that we offer on behalf of our brothers and sisters who are ill. Increase their faith and trust in you. Comfort them with your loving presence and, if it is your will, give them back their health, give them new strength in body and soul.

O loving Father, bless those who are dying, bless all those who will soon meet you face to face. We believe that you have made death the door to eternal life. Sustain in your name our brothers and sisters who are at the end of their lives, and bring them safely home into eternal life with you.

O God, the source of all power, defend and protect those who take care of the sick and tend the dying. Give them a courageous and gentle spirit. Support them in their efforts to provide comfort and relief. Make them a radiant sign of your transfiguring love.

Lord of life and foundation of our hope, pour your abundant blessings on all those who live and work and die. Fill them with your peace and your grace. Show them that you are a loving Father, a God of mercy and compassion. Amen.

FEBRUARY 3, 1986

May your spirit descend

Lord,
let us speak
all the languages of the modern world:
of culture and civilization,
of social, economic,
and political renewal,
of justice and liberation,
of information,
and of social communication.
Let us proclaim everywhere
and in every thing
your great works.
May your Spirit descend!
Renew the face of the earth,
through the revelation of the children
  of God.

REGINA COELI, MAY 18, 1986

Giving thanks for the Virgin Mary

Thank you, O Christ, for giving us your Mother. With the words that you uttered on the Cross, "Behold your Son," you entrusted her into the hands of John, so that she might be the mother of all men.

We praise you, Lord, because you show your immense grandeur in the humility of your servant. You chose her and adorned her with all the graces, raised her above the angels and the saints, so that our Holy Mother Mary, full of grace, would be the "wonder" of God, she whom this entire nation of Chile hails with love and filial gratitude.

"Let every living creature praise the Lord." With the powerful aid of your Mother, O Lord, we wish to spread over all the earth the fruits of your Covenant of love with man. We want all men to recognize you and praise you as the Lord and Creator; to be able to discover your presence in their lives and the purpose for which they were created; to strive to make the image that you, with loving kindness, have impressed in their hearts shine forth. With your grace insure that the divine image carved in their souls is not obscured by hatred and violence against life, especially against life that is already conceived and not yet born; that it is not dimmed by the perversion of habits or the illusory escapes of drugs and sexual disorders; that it is not abandoned to the pressures of materialistic ideologies, of any sort, which strike and cut off at the root the very dignity of the individual.

Today we ask, O Lord, that all who have stopped praising you by choosing paths that lead away from the Gospel may abandon those ways and return to you through the Virgin Mary.

And you, good Mother, who are always near your children, who patiently await their return to the Church, bring them back! We beg God for your intercession!

APRIL 5, 1987

Sustain us in unity

O God,
who by means of water
and the Holy Spirit
have caused us to be reborn to eternal life
in the new creation,
in your bounty continue
to pour your blessings
on all your sons and daughters;
defend us always,
wherever we may be,
among the faithful, your people,
united by our common baptism
and confessing together the only faith
inherited by the Apostles,
in order to bear witness
in a divided world
and to seek the full unity
willed by Christ through his Church.
He is God
and lives and reigns with you
in the unity of the Holy Spirit
for ever and ever.

JANUARY 21, 1987

God of our daily work

"You are blessed, God of the universe." *Yes, blessed are you, Lord. God of our families!* God of our daily work. God of our joys and of our sorrows!

We pray to you for all those who suffer, for those who have no money, those who have no education, those who are in need of affection: make us attentive to their wants and teach us to share.

We pray to you for the unemployed and for young people who are looking for work: help us to prepare a place for them in our society.

We pray to you for the sick, for those who have lost all hope of getting well, for those who are nearing death: sustain them, comfort them, console them, give them patience and serenity.

We pray to you for those in this nation who are hungry, for those who are exiled, for refugees. Lord, master of the impossible, put an end to our sorrows, expand our hearts, and bring us together in unity.

Finally, *we pray to you and glorify you* for all our brothers and sisters in the world, in whom we find your face!

We pray to you and glorify you for families, and especially those which give up to you a life from their home!

SEPTEMBER 9, 1990

Support the Church

O Heavenly Father, rich in mercy, you who have filled all men with the mystery of your infinite love, sustain the Church of your only Son. Make these days a time of benediction and salvation for her, a moment of openness and reconciliation, a moment of faith and hope in the very heart of the storm, since you are omnipotent and full of mercy.

O Jesus Christ, our God, our Savior, and our hope, you who founded the Church, the sign of salvation for the generations into eternity, visit her with your victorious Cross so that the forces of Hell will not have dominion over her. Enlighten her with your word; guide her in knowledge; renew her with the teaching of your Gospel and with the force of the Holy Spirit. Confirm her solidly in faith; nourish her with your bread, the bread of truth; bind her sons with the chains of charity and harmony so that she may live in you and be a witness to your love. Glory to you forever.

O Holy Spirit, Spirit of the Father and of the Son, the dispenser of charisms, you who dwell in the Church and make of her a holy temple, fill us with the infinite variety of your gifts so that we may be living members helping each other to build the Holy Church. Be our comforter, our guide, and our strength. Make us worthy of the name of Christians, by which we are called to render testimony of Christ and the value of his Gospel, permeating our society with it.

Thus, after long suffering, in the very cradle of the diversity of our confessions, we will be fully conscious of being brothers and sisters together. Praise to you forever.

O Virgin Mary, Mother of God and our Mother, who accompanied our people at the different stages of their life and guarded them in the faith, we turn to you; we place our path under your protection and entrust it to your maternal care, so that you may help us receive the breath of the Spirit and call on your Son to guide us. We honor you forever.

JUNE 20, 1992

Guide us in all our works

God, you are our Creator.
You are good and your mercy has no limits.
Every creature praises you.
O God, you have given us an inner law by which we must live.
Doing your will means fulfilling our duty.
To follow your paths means to know peace in our souls.
To you we offer our obedience.
Guide us in all the works that we initiate on earth.
Deliver us from evil tendencies that lead our hearts away from your will.
Do not allow us to distance ourselves from you.
O God, judge of all humanity, help us to be among your elect on the last day.
God, author of justice and peace, grant us true joy, authentic love, and a lasting solidarity among peoples.
Fill us with your gifts forever.
Amen!

FEBRUARY 22, 1992

Most Holy Trinity, blessed and the source of all blessedness, bless your sons and daughters whom you have called to praise the greatness of your love, your merciful goodness, and your beauty.

Father most holy, sanctify the sons and daughters who have consecrated themselves to you for the glory of your name. Enfold them with your power, enabling them to bear witness that you are the origin of all things, the one source of love and freedom. We thank you for the gift of the consecrated life, which in faith seeks you and in its universal mission invites all people to draw near to you.

Jesus our Savior, Word Incarnate, as you have entrusted your own way of life to those whom you have called, continue to draw to yourself men and women who will be, for the people of our time, dispensers of mercy, heralds of your return, living signs of the Resurrection and of its treasures of virginity, poverty, and obedience. May no tribulation separate them from you and from your love!

Holy Spirit, love poured into our hearts, who grant grace and inspiration to our minds, the perennial source of life, who bring to fulfillment the mission of Christ by means of many charisms, we pray to you for all consecrated persons. Fill their hearts with the deep certainty of having been chosen to love, to praise, and to serve. Enable them to savor your friendship, fill them with your joy and consolation, help them to overcome moments of difficulty and to rise up again with trust after they have fallen; make them mirrors of the divine beauty. Give them the courage to face the challenges of our time and the grace to bring to all mankind the goodness and loving kindness of our Savior Jesus Christ.

VITA CONSECRATA, III

(APOSTOLIC EXHORTATION, MARCH 25, 1996)

Our Father who is in Heaven

Holy Father, friend of all creatures,
everlastingly in your Word
you loved us and thought of us
and wished us to recognize your face
in the face of your Only Begotten
born of Mary.
In him, tested in everything, like us,
except sin,
you suffered our weaknesses;
in him your mercy extends
from generation to generation forever.
Holy Father,
see your people
as, after celebrating the memory
of the Passion and death of the Lord,
they follow the Way of the Cross,
praying in expectation of the Resurrection.
We share your Son's cry of pain,
its echo continuing in the cry
that goes up from the countless crosses
of men and women of all epochs.
We are in communion
with his offering of love,
while his Passion draws to a close:
in the tragic period
of suffering and death
we pray that the trusting dialogue of us children

with you, Father,
in the Spirit of your Son
may never cease.
He lives and reigns forever and ever.

INITIAL PRAYER OF THE
VIA CRUCIS, APRIL 2, 1999

Help us to love men

God, our Father,
in Jesus, your Son,
you have welcomed all men
as your children.
He became a brother and a friend to all,
especially the poor
and the dispossessed.
Look upon the many men and women,
everywhere in the world,
who are despised;
look at the many
who are forced to live
in ways unworthy of man.
We pray to you, Father of all men,
deliver the world from the evil of selfishness
and violence.
Help us to love men
as you love them:
unconditionally and without limits.
Hear our prayer
through Jesus Christ, your Son,
our Lord and God,
who lives and reigns with you
in the unity of the Holy Spirit
forever and ever.
Amen.

GERMANY, JUNE 23, 1996

Prayer for the third year of preparation for the Great Jubilee of 2000

Blessed are you, Lord,
Father in Heaven,
because in your infinite mercy
you looked down on man's wretchedness
and gave us Jesus, your Son,
born of woman,
our Savior and friend,
brother and Redeemer.
Thank you, good Father,
for the gift of the Jubilee year;
let it be a favorable time,
the year of the great return to our Father's house,
where you, full of love,
await your lost children
to give them the embrace of forgiveness
and welcome them to your table,
clothed in holiday garments.

To you, Father, our eternal praise!

Most merciful Father,
in the Holy Year
may love for you flourish vigorously,
and for our neighbor, too:
may the disciples of Christ
promote justice and peace;

may the Good News
be proclaimed to the poor,
and let Mother Church direct
her preferential love
to the poor and the outcast.

To you, Father, our eternal praise!

Righteous Father,
may the great Jubilee be a propitious occasion
for all Catholics to rediscover the joy
of living attentive to your Word
and abandoned to your will;
may they feel the value
of fraternal communion,
breaking bread together
and praising you with hymns and spiritual songs.

To you, Father, our eternal praise!

O Father, rich in mercy,
may the Holy Jubilee be a time of openness,
of dialogue and meeting
among all the believers in Christ
and the followers of other religions.
In your immense love
be generous with mercy for all.

To you, Father, our eternal praise!

. . .

O God, Almighty Father,
let all your children know
that gentle Most Holy Mary accompanies
them on the road to you,
man's final destination:
she who is the icon of pure love,
chosen by you to be
the Mother of Christ and of the Church.

To you, Father, our eternal praise!

To you, Father of life,
the principle without principle,
the highest goodness and the eternal light,
with the Son and with the Spirit,
honor and glory, praise and gratitude,
to the end of time.
Amen.

For the celebration of the Great Jubilee of the year 2000

Blessed are you, O Father,
who in your infinite love
gave us your Only Begotten Son,
made flesh through the action of the Holy Spirit
in the pure womb of the Virgin Mary,
and born in Bethlehem two thousand years ago.

Praise and glory to you, Most Holy Trinity, you alone are God Most High!

He became our traveling companion
and gave new meaning to history,
which is a road taken together
in hardship and in suffering,
in faithfulness and in love,
toward the new heavens and the new earth,
where you, when death has been vanquished, will be all in all.

Praise and glory to you, Most Holy Trinity, you alone are God Most High!

With the force of the Spirit, O Father, sustain
the commitment of the Church
to the new evangelization,
and guide our steps on the paths of the world,
so that we may proclaim Christ with our life
by directing our earthly pilgrimage

toward the City of Light.
May the disciples of Jesus be radiant
in their love
for the poor and the oppressed;
may they feel solidarity with the needy
and be generous in works of mercy;
may they be indulgent toward their brothers and sisters
so that they themselves may obtain from you
indulgence and forgiveness.

Praise and glory to you, Most Holy Trinity, you alone are God Most High!

Grant, Father,
that the disciples of your Son,
purifying their memory
and recognizing their own sins,
may be one,
so that the world will believe.
May the dialogue
between the followers of the great religions spread,
and all men discover the joy
of being your children.
May the voices of the Apostles
and the Christian martyrs,
of the righteous among every people and of every era,
be joined in prayer
with the supplicant voice of Mary,
Mother of peoples,
so that the Holy Year may be

a reason for renewed hope
and joy in the Spirit
for individuals and for the Church.

Praise and glory to you, Most Holy Trinity, you alone are God Most High!

To you, Almighty Father,
creator of the cosmos and of man,
through Christ, the living one,
the Lord of time and history,
in the Spirit that makes all things holy,
praise, honor, and glory
today and forever world without end.
Amen!

To Christ

The Redeemer of man,
Jesus Christ is the center of the universe and of history.
To him go my thoughts
and my heart in this solemn hour.

Redemptor Hominis
(Encyclical, March 4, 1979)

Lead us into truth

Lord, show us the way!

Lead me into truth! Lead us into truth!

Lead into truth, O Christ, *the mothers and fathers* of the parish: spurred and fortified by the Sacramental Grace of marriage, and conscious of being on earth the visible sign of your perfect love for the Church, may they be serene and decisive in facing, with the consistency of the Gospel, the responsibilities of conjugal life and of the Christian education of their children.

Lead into truth, O Christ, *the young people* of the parish: let them not be attracted by new idols, such as consumerism, well-being at any cost, moral permissiveness, violent protest, but let them live your message with joy, which is the message of the beatitudes, the message of love for God and for one's neighbor, the message of a moral commitment to the genuine transformation of society.

Lead into truth, O Christ, *all the faithful* of the parish: may Christian faith animate their whole life and make them courageous witnesses before the world of your mission of salvation, conscientious and energetic members of the Church, joyful children of God, and brothers and sisters, with you, of all men!

Show us, O Christ, the way of truth! Forever!

DECEMBER 2, 1979

Holy Friday

Christ Jesus! We are about to conclude this Holy Day of Holy Friday at the foot of your Cross. Just as long ago in Jerusalem your Mother, John, and Magdalene and other women stood at the foot of the Cross, so, too, we are here. We are profoundly moved by the importance of the moment. Words fail us in expressing all that our hearts feel. On this night—when, after taking you down from the Cross, they laid you in a tomb at the foot of Calvary—we wish to pray *that you will remain with us by way of your Cross:* you, who through the Cross separated yourself from us. We pray that you will remain with the Church; that you will remain with humanity; that you will not be dismayed if many, perhaps, pass by your Cross indifferently, if some keep their distance from it, and others do not get there.

And yet perhaps never more than today has man needed this power and this knowledge that you yourself are, you alone: by means of your Cross.

Then stay with us in this penetrating mystery of your death, in which you revealed how much "God loved the world." Stay with us and draw us to you, you who fell beneath this Cross. Stay with us through your Mother, to whom you, from the Cross, entrusted every man in particular.

Abide with us!

Stat Crux, dum volvitur orbis! Yes, "the Cross remains constant while the world turns!"

APRIL 11, 1979

O Christ,
let all that is part
of today's meeting
originate in the Spirit of truth
and *be made fruitful* through love.
Look before us:
the past and the future!
Look before us:
the desire of so many hearts!
You,
who are the Lord of history
and the Lord of human hearts,
be with us!
Jesus Christ
eternal Son of God,
be with us!
Amen.

MAY 29, 1982

"Lord, stay with us"

"Lord, stay with us."

The Disciples said these words for the first time in Emmaus. Later, in the course of centuries, they have been on the lips of so many of your disciples and confessors, innumerable times, O Christ.

I utter the same words, *to call on you*, Christ, in your Eucharistic presence, to welcome the daily worship lasting through the entire day, in this temple.

Stay with us today, and stay, from now on, every day.

Stay! So that we may *meet you* in the prayer of adoration and thanks, in the prayer of expiation and petition.

Stay! You who are at the same time *veiled* in the Eucharistic mystery of faith and *unveiled* under the species of bread and wine, which you have assumed in this Sacrament.

Stay! So that you may ceaselessly reconfirm your presence in this temple, and all those who enter may know that it is your house, "the dwelling of God among men," and find the very source of life and holiness that pours from your Eucharistic heart.

The Eucharist is the sacramental testimony of *your First Coming*, by which the words of the prophets have been confirmed and their expectations fulfilled. You left us, O Lord, your Body and your Blood under the species of bread and wine so that they might attest to the redemption of the world as it transpired—so that through them your Paschal Mystery might reach all men, as the Sacrament of Life and salvation. At the same time, the Eucharist is a steadfast herald of *your*

Second Coming and the sign of the ultimate Advent and the expectation of the whole Church: *"We announce your death, Lord, we proclaim your Resurrection, in expectation of your Coming."*

We long to worship you every day and every hour, stripped under the "species of bread and wine," to renew the hope of the *"call to glory"* whose beginning you established with your body glorified *"at the right hand of the Father."*

One day, O Lord, you asked Peter: *"Do you love me?"*

You asked him three times—and three times the Apostle answered: *"Lord, you know everything; you know that I love you." Peter's answer* is expressed *through* this adoration every day and all day.

All who participate in the adoration of your Eucharistic presence bear witness every time they do so, and make the truth contained in the words of the Apostle resound again: "Lord, you know everything; *you know that I love you."*

Amen.

INAUGURATION OF THE PERMANENT EXHIBITION OF THE EUCHARIST AT ST. PETER'S, DECEMBER 2, 1981

O Christ the Savior

O Christ the Savior, we give thanks to you for your redeeming sacrifice, the unique hope of men and women!

O Christ the Savior, we give thanks to you for the Eucharistic breaking of the Bread, which you instituted in order to meet in reality your brothers and sisters during the course of the centuries!

O Christ the Savior, instill in the hearts of the baptized the desire to offer themselves with you and to pledge themselves to the salvation of their brothers and sisters!

You who are actually present in the Holy Sacrament, pour your blessings abundantly on your assembled people, so that you may remain a true sign of the new world!

Amen.

JULY 21, 1981

Eucharistic Worship

Lord Jesus,
we appear before you,
knowing that you call us
and that you love us just as we are.
"You have the words of eternal life;
and we have believed, and have come to know,
that you are the Holy One of God."
Through you and the Holy Spirit
who communicates to us,
we wish to reach the Father
to say to him our "Yes" joined to yours.
With you we can now say:
"Our Father."
Following you, *"the Way, the Truth, and the Life,"*
we wish to penetrate the apparent
"silence" and "absence" of God,
tearing the cloud of Tabor
to listen to the voice of the Father who says:
"This is my beloved Son,
in whom I am well pleased.
Listen to him."

With this faith made of contemplative listening,
we will be able to shed light on our personal
circumstances and, similarly, on the various areas
of family life and the life of society.

. . .

We long to have your feelings
and see things as you see them,
because you are the center,
the beginning and the end of everything.
Supported by this hope,
we wish to instill in the world
this hierarchy of evangelical values,
through which God and his gifts of salvation
occupy the most important place in the heart
and actions of concrete life.

We wish to love as you love,
you who give life and communicate yourself
with all that you are.
We would like to be able to say with St. Paul:
"For me to live is Christ."
Without you our life has no meaning.

We wish to learn
"to be with the one we know loves us"
because *"with such a good friend present
one can endure anything."*
In you we learn to become one with
the will of the Father,
because, in prayer, *"to speak is love."*

Entering into your intimacy,
we wish to assume important
resolutions and attitudes,
make lasting decisions and

fundamental choices in accordance
with our own Christian vocation.

Believing, hoping, and loving,
we worship you in a simple spirit
of presence, silence, and expectation,
which will also be reparation,
in response to your words:
"Stay here and watch with me."
You overcome the poverty of our thoughts,
feelings, and words;
for this reason we wish to learn to worship
by admiring your mystery,
loving it just as it is and being silent
with a friendly silence
and a giving presence.

If you are present
in our physical and moral nights,
you love us and talk to us,
and that is enough for us, despite the fact that, many times,
we are not aware of the consolation.

By learning this dimension of worship,
we will be in your intimacy or "mystery";
then our prayer
will turn out of respect toward the "mystery"
of every brother and every event
in order to insert us into the environment of
our family and society,

and build history
with this active and fruitful silence
which begins in contemplation.

Thanks to you,
our capacity for silence
and worship will be transformed
into the capacity to love and serve.
You have given us your Mother as our mother,
so that she may teach us to meditate
and worship in our hearts.
She, accepting the Word
and putting it into practice,
became the most perfect Mother.

Help us to be your missionary Church
that knows how to meditate on your Word,
in adoration and love,
in order to transform it into life
and communicate it to all our brothers and sisters.
Amen.

DECEMBER 31, 1982

Man's Redeemer

"My eyes have seen your salvation, which you have prepared before all the people: light to illuminate the peoples and the glory of your people of Israel."

Yes. My eyes see *your salvation.* They see in you the salvation of man and of the world, Jesus Christ, born in Bethlehem, Redeemer of mankind and the world!

My eyes see salvation in you. You are all the hope of my life, just as you have been the hope of the generations of Israel. For you I have lived up to now—and for you I will live from this moment on. You are *the faith, the hope, and the love* of my heart, of all my actions, aspirations, and desires.

FEBRUARY 2, 1983

We give thanks to you, O Christ!

We give thanks to you, O Christ!

We give thanks to you, because in the Eucharist you receive us, though we are unworthy, through the power of the Holy Spirit in the unity of your Body and your Blood, in the unity of your Death and your Resurrection!

We give thanks to you, O Christ!

We give thanks to you, because you allow the Church to be constantly reborn on this earth and because you allow her *to bring forth sons and daughters* of this earth as adopted children of God and heirs of eternal destinies.

Accept the thanks of our community. O Christ! We pray to you to be among us, as on the night of Easter you were among the Apostles at the Last Supper; we implore you to say yet again:

"As the Father has sent me, even so I send you."

And give to these words the powerful breath of Pentecost.

Make us faithful to these words!

Let us be *wherever you send us... because the Father sent you.*

NATIONAL EUCHARISTIC CONGRESS,
MILAN, MAY 22, 1983

The Lord of all history

Jesus Christ, the Son of the living God, / who took your body from the Virgin Mary / and became man through the action of the Holy Spirit! / Jesus Christ, Redeemer of man! / You who are the same yesterday and today and through the centuries! Welcome this extraordinary Jubilee year / that your Church offers / in celebration of the nineteen-hundred-and-fiftieth anniversary of your Death and Resurrection / for the redemption of the world. / You, who through the act of Redemption created the source / of a gift for your earthly Bride that is always new, / make her salvific force *penetrate* during all the days, / weeks, and months of this year, / so that it may become for us truly / "the year of the Lord's Grace."

May we all in this time / *love you* even more, renewing in ourselves/ the mysteries of your life, / from conception and birth / to the Cross and the Resurrection. / Be with us through these mysteries, / be with us in the Holy Spirit, / do not leave us orphans!/ Always come back to us.

Let *all turn to love,* / seeing in you, Son of eternal love, / the Father who is "rich in mercy." / In the course of this year let the entire Church / feel the abundance of your redemption, / which is manifested in the remission of sins, / and purification from their remains, / which weigh on souls called to immortal life. / Help us to overcome our indifference and our sloth! / Give us the consciousness of sin. / Create in us, O Lord, a pure heart, / and renew a strong spirit / in our conscience.

O Lord, let this holy year / of your Redemption also become / *an appeal to the modern world,* / that sees justice and peace / on the horizon of its desires / —and yet, giving more and more space to sin, / lives, day by day, in the midst of / increasing tensions and threats, / and seems / to be moving / in a direction dangerous for all! / Help us change the direction / of the ever-increasing threats / and misfortunes of the modern world! / Rouse man! / Protect nations and peoples! Do not allow the acts of destruction / that threaten humanity today!

O Lord Jesus Christ, / *may the work of your Redemption appear more powerful!* / The Church implores you / in this year, through your Mother, / whom you gave to be the *Mother of all men.* / The Church implores you / in the mystery of the *communion of the Saints.* / The Church implores you insistently: O Christ! / May the work of your Redemption / —in man and in the world— / show itself to be more powerful! / Amen.

OPENING OF THE HOLY DOOR,
MARCH 25, 1983

Praise to you, on the threshold of the Holy Year

Praise to you—Word of God!

Praise to you, eternal Word, who becomes flesh in the womb of the Immaculate Virgin through the action of the Holy Spirit.

Praise to you, Word—*Only Begotten Son of the Eternal Father*—who, by your Incarnation, initiate the Redemption of the world. Behold, in your Incarnation the prospect of the Cross and the Resurrection already opens up. *Ave Crux. O Crux, ave, spes unica!* Hail to the Cross. O Cross, hail, our only hope!

Praise to you, *Son of Man!* Behold, your joy is to dwell "among the sons of man" and "proclaim" to them the hour of their salvation. Praise to you, on the threshold of this new time! *Praise to you, on the threshold of the Holy Year of Redemption!*

ANGELUS,
MARCH 20, 1983

Stay with us

Lord,
the day is already waning,
stay with us.
Stay to illuminate our doubts
and our fears.
Stay so that we may fortify
our light with yours.
Stay to help us be
strong and generous.
Stay so that in a world
that has little faith and hope
we may be able to encourage
one another
and sow faith and hope.
Stay
so that we, too, may learn from you
to be the light for other young people
and for the world.

APRIL 11, 1984

Let this prayer be a bulwark for all of you, dear brothers and sisters:

may it help your generation and the generations that follow to know God more profoundly;

may "the eyes of your heart" be enlightened, so that nothing disturbs you or blinds you;

may you be increasingly aware of "what is the hope to which he has called you";

may you understand "what are the riches of the glorious inheritance" which Christ left us, through the birth of the Virgin Mary;

may it enable you to discover "what is the immeasurable greatness of his power in us who believe": that power which was manifested by his Resurrection and his Ascension.

Jesus Christ: true Son of God! Jesus Christ: true man, who sits "at the right hand of God."

So let it be.

O Lord Christ, chosen Son of the Father, / friend of man, Teacher who loves life, / you forget no creature.

Look at the Church; / pour into her the life-giving breath and fire of your Spirit. / Impress on her the seal of the Holy Spirit, / remind the baptized that they are members of your body. / Dwell in their hearts with faith. / Let them find their roots and their foundation in love. / Open them to the praise of your glory.

O Christ Lord, power and knowledge of God, / you will lead everything to its fulfillment, / because the power of your love surpasses all knowledge; / you can give us more than we know how to ask for.

Give your people the spirit of wisdom, / enlighten the eyes of their hearts / so that they may welcome your Word as the leaven of their whole life: / of the family and society, of work and free time, / of infancy and youth, / of adulthood and old age.

O Christ, wisdom of God, / shining reflection of his glory and expression of his being, / you sustain the universe with the power of your Word. / Teach this people the true meaning of the things of this world / and the love of eternal goods, so that it may be able to employ your gifts,/ distinguishing good and evil.

Give this people love within families, / justice in social relations, / truth in the means of communication, / reconciliation of conflicts. / Help the men of this nation to make use of their time, / to serve your Father and all their brothers and sisters, to love one another against the forces of evil, / and to live as children of light.

O Christ, Son of God, / you emptied yourself, taking the form of a servant, / and being born in the likeness of man humbled yourself until your death on the Cross. / Firstborn among the dead, risen Christ, / through you it pleased the Father to reconcile all beings. / Through our baptism in your Death and your Resurrection, / you allow us, too, to live a new life.

By way of the Virgin Mary, your Mother with an immaculate heart, / we pray to you: / enable us to discover the treasure of wisdom hidden in you. / With Mary, we wish to keep it and ponder it in our hearts. / With Mary, who was present among the Disciples, / grant that we may be faithful witnesses, / in faith and in love. Amen.

MAY 10, 1985

"Everyone is searching for you," *O Jesus Christ*

Yes, "everyone is searching for you," O Jesus Christ!

Many search for you *directly,* calling you by name, with faith, hope and charity.

There are some who search for you *indirectly:* through others.

And there are some who *search for you* without knowing it...

And there are also those who search for you even though they deny that they are doing so.

Nevertheless, all men are searching for you, and they are searching for you above all because *you search for them first;* because *you became man for all men,* in the womb of the Virgin Mother; because *you redeemed all men* at the cost of your Cross.

In this way *you opened,* among the tangled and impassable paths of the human heart and the destiny of man, *the way.*

To you, who are the way, the truth, and the life, we turn in this prayer through the heart of your Mother, the Virgin, most Holy Mary.

ANGELUS, FEBRUARY 10, 1985

Eucharistic worship

Lord Jesus,
we are gathered here before you.
You are the Son of God made man,
crucified by us and raised up by the Father.
You, the living one,
actually present among us.
You, the way, the truth, and the life:
you, who alone have words of eternal life.
You, the sole foundation of our salvation
and the sole name to invoke
if we are to have hope.
You, the image of the Father
and the giver of the Spirit;
you, Love: Love not loved!
Lord Jesus, we believe in you,
we worship you,
we love you with all our heart,
and we proclaim your name above every other name.

In this solemn moment
we pray to you for our city.
Watch over it, O Christ, from your Cross,
and save it.
Watch over the poor, the sick,
the old people, the outcast,
the young men and girls
who have embarked on desperate roads,

the many families in trouble and afflicted by misfortune
and society's ills.
Look, and have pity!
Look at those who no longer know how to believe
in the Father who is in Heaven,
who no longer perceive his tenderness,
those who cannot
read in your face,
O Crucified One,
their pain, their poverty,
and their sufferings.
See how many are lying in sin,
far from you,
who are the source of living water:
the only one who takes away thirst
and soothes the yearning and restless anxiety
of the human heart.
Look at them and have pity!

Bless our city and our neighborhood.
Bless all the workers
who by their daily toil
see to the needs of families
and the progress of society.
Bless the young,
so that hope of a better world
is not extinguished in their hearts,
nor the wish to devote themselves generously
to build it.
Bless those who govern us,

that they may work for justice and peace.
Bless the priests
who lead the communities,
the men and women religious, the consecrated.
Bless the seminary and give to the diocese
generous young men and women
willing to accept the call
to give themselves completely to the service of the Gospel
and their brothers and sisters.

O Lord Jesus, allow
our parish community
to be confirmed
in the faith of baptism,
so that it may possess the joy of the truth,
the only road that leads to life!
Give it the grace of reconciliation
that spills from your pierced heart,
O Crucified One:
so that, reconciled and united,
it may become a force
that transcends divisions,
and, leavened by a new mentality
of solidarity and sharing,
is a living call to follow you
who became the brother of us all.
Finally, let it be a community that is a
messenger of hope for all men and women,
and may this testimony of hope
spur them to commit themselves,

to work for a
more united and peaceful world,
conforming to the will of your Father,
our Creator.

Lord Jesus
give us peace, you who are peace
and on your Cross transcended every division.
And make us
true workers for peace and justice:
men and women
who are committed to build
a world that is more just,
more united, and more fraternal.
Lord Jesus,
return among us
and make us vigilant
in expectation of your coming.
Amen.

June 16, 1985

"Thanks for what you are and for what you do"

Lord Jesus Christ, the Redeemer of human beings, we turn to your Sacred Heart with humility and honesty, with veneration and hope, with a deep desire to give you glory, honor, and praise.

Lord Jesus Christ, Savior of the world, we thank you for all that you are and for all that you do for your little flock.

Lord Jesus Christ, son of the living God, we praise you for the love that you have revealed with your Sacred Heart, that was pierced for us and became the source of our joy, the origin of our eternal life.

Gathered together in your name, which is more exalted than other names, we dedicate ourselves to your Sacred Heart, in which the fullness of truth and charity resides.

In dedicating ourselves to you, we renew the desire to repay with love the rich manifestation of your merciful love.

Lord Jesus Christ, King of Love and Prince of Peace, reign in our hearts and in our houses. Drive out the powers of evil and let us share the victory of your Sacred Heart. All of us speak and give glory and praise to you, to the Father, and to the Holy Spirit, the only living God who will reign forever. Amen.

FEBRUARY 2, 1986

O Good Shepherd

"Lord, you know everything; you know that I love you."

"Even though I walk in the valley of the shadow of death, yet I fear no evil, because thou art with me."

You who are the Shepherd, the Eternal Shepherd, the Good Shepherd, *the Shepherd of all human vocations* and all the ways of humanity.

You who go in search of those who are lost. . . . You who bring back to the fold those who have strayed . . . you who heal the wounds of those who are injured and take care of those who are feeble and sick.

Do not let human beings get lost on the wrong road, the blind alley, *looking out only for themselves,* their own possibilities and achievements!

Make them *understand* that you are the Shepherd, the Good Shepherd who offered his life for each one of us!

Let us search for your hand to guide us; and find in you the way, the truth, and the life!

OCTOBER 10, 1988

Enable us to understand the Scriptures

This Church, animated by the Spirit of Consolation, needs you, Lord, to look ahead with optimism, sustained by the certainty of your presence.

You, who are risen, walk with her!

Let the hearts of those who believe in you, who seek you, and who dedicate themselves to the proclamation of your truth be ardent.

Show us again today the road that we must travel and assure your flock of the supernatural aid of your grace.

Stand beside our priests so that they may serve the Gospel everywhere, all the time! Do not let them be discouraged by tribulation, dispirited by solitude, or worn down by hardships.

Speak to the hearts of consecrated souls; sustain those who on the frontiers of charity proclaim your mercy to the lowliest and most wretched. Comfort them with the Word that gives peace.

Lord, enable those whom you send as messengers of the truth and the life in the family, in culture, in society, and in politics to understand the Scriptures. Let the hearts of the young be fervent while you give spiritual strength to their fresh and generous energies. Your call to evangelize is for all.

Lord Jesus, enable us to understand the Scriptures; let our hearts be ardent while you speak to us. Amen.

APRIL 28, 1991

Eucharist and community

Lord Jesus, who in the Eucharist placed your dwelling among us and became a traveler with us, sustain *our Christian communities,* so that they may become more open to hearing your Word and accepting it. Let them get from the Eucharist a renewed commitment to proclaim your Gospel and so disseminate the signs and gestures of an attentive and hardworking charity throughout society.

Lord Jesus, in your Eucharist let Christian spouses be "signs" among us of your sponsal love; let *families* be communities of persons who, living in dialogue with God and among themselves, do not fear life and become seedbeds of priestly, religious, and missionary vocations.

Lord Jesus, from your altar radiate light and grace upon *this city,* so that, by rejecting the seduction of a materialistic conception of life, it may defeat the selfishness that besieges it, the injustice that distresses it, the divisions that afflict it.

Lord Jesus: give us your joy, give us your peace.

Stay with us, Lord!

You alone have the words of eternal life.

JUNE 21, 1992

Prayer for families

Lord Jesus, we thank you because the Gospel of the Father's love, with which you came to save the world, has been proclaimed far and wide in America, as a gift of the Holy Spirit that fills us with gladness.

We thank you for the gift of your life, which you gave us by loving us to the end: it makes us children of God and brothers and sisters of each other. Increase our faith and our love for you, Lord, who are present in the many tabernacles of the continent.

Grant that we may be faithful witnesses to your Resurrection for the younger generations, so that knowing you they may follow you and find in you their peace and joy. Only then will they know that they are brothers and sisters of all God's children, scattered throughout the world. You, who, in becoming man, chose to belong to a human family, teach families the virtues that filled the house in Nazareth with light. May families always be united, as you and the Father are one, and be living witnesses to love, justice, and solidarity; make them schools of respect, forgiveness, and mutual help, so that the world may believe; help them to be a source of vocations to the priesthood, to the consecrated life, and all other forms of firm Christian commitment.

Protect your Church and the successor of Peter, to whom you, Good Shepherd, have entrusted the task of feeding your flock. Grant that your Church may flourish and grow richer in the fruits of holiness. Teach us to love your Mother, Mary, as you loved her. Give us the strength to proclaim your Word with courage in the work of the new evangelization, so that the world may know new hope.

Ecclesia in America
(Apostolic Exhortation,
January 26, 1999)

Prayer for the first year of preparation for the Great Jubilee of 2000

Lord Jesus,
Lord of time and Lord of history,
make our souls eager
to celebrate with faith
the Great Jubilee of 2000,
so that it may be a year of grace and mercy.
Give us a humble and simple heart,
so that we may contemplate
with ever-renewed wonder
the mystery of the Incarnation,
when you, the Son of the Most High,
in the womb of the Virgin,
sanctuary of the Spirit,
became our Brother.

*Praise and glory to you, O Christ,
today and for all eternity.*

Jesus, the beginning and end
of the new man,
turn our hearts toward you,
so that, having abandoned the paths of error,
we may walk in your footsteps
on the road that leads to life.
Help us to be faithful to the promises of baptism,
to live our faith consistently,

bearing forceful witness to your word,
so that in the family and in society the vivifying light of the Gospel may shine.

Praise and glory to you, O Christ,
today and for all eternity.

Jesus, power and wisdom of God,
kindle in us love
for the divine Scripture,
where the voice of the Father resounds,
which enlightens and inflames, nourishes and comforts.
You, the Word of the living God,
renew the Church's missionary impulse,
so that all people may arrive at
knowledge of you,
the true Son of God and true Son of man,
the only Mediator between man and God.

Praise and glory to you, O Christ,
today and for all eternity.

Jesus, who are the source of unity and peace,
strengthen the communion in your Church,
give impetus to the ecumenical movement,
so that all your disciples,
with the force of your Spirit,
may become one.
You who gave us as a standard of life
the new commandment of love,

make us builders of a strong world,
in which war is vanquished by peace,
the culture of death
by the commitment to life.

Praise and glory to you, O Christ,
today and for all eternity.

Jesus, Only Begotten Son of the Father,
full of grace and truth,
the light that illuminates every man,
to those who seek you with a sincere heart
give the abundance of your life.
To you, man's Redeemer,
the beginning and the end of time and the cosmos,
to the Father, the inexhaustible Creator of every good,
to the Holy Spirit, the seal of infinite love,
all honor and glory through eternity.
Amen.

To the Holy Spirit

The Church . . . ,
drawing on the experience of the Pentecost . . .
has proclaimed since the earliest centuries
her faith
in the Holy Spirit
as the giver of life.

DOMINUM ET VIVIFICANTEM
(ENCYCLICAL, MAY 18, 1986)

"O Spirit, O Consoler"

We praise and thank you for this *effusion of the Spirit* upon the apostolic Church which is in Rome, the Church of the end of the second millennium.

We thank you for the Second Vatican Council, which became a guide in the work of the synods. We thank you for the sons and daughters of God's people who—as the prophet Joel says—"will prophesy": we thank you for the sons and daughters of our Church, to whom the gift of light and counsel has been given, as *participants in the prophetic vocation* to serve the divine truth, the *Gospel of salvation for all the generations.*

O Consoling Spirit / Spirit of the Father and the Son / descend and renew the face of the earth! / May your strength penetrate us all / so that the countenance of this Church may be renewed.

"Let us not despair..."

Behold, out of the distant past, the image of that city and that tower appears—the tower of Babel, from which we inherited divisions and quarrels, *when men began to build against God.* "So the LORD scattered them abroad from there over the face of all the earth, and they left off building the city." Let us not despair.

O Holy Spirit God, Spirit of the Pentecost, come and dwell among us. Guide us on that road of communion, on which we set forth during the years of the Synod...

"Let us not despair!"

. . .

"Mentes tuorum visita..."

"Visit the souls of those who belong to you, fill with your grace from on high the hearts which you have made."

"Come, come, Holy Spirit! Amen."

May 29, 1993

Holy Spirit, we appear before you as sinners, but gathered together in your name. Come among us, stay with us, enter into our hearts, teach us what to do and what direction to take. Show us what to choose so that, with your help, we may please you in all things. Be our counselor and the author of our purposes; you who with God the Father and his Son bear the name of glorious; you who love justice, do not let us become its destroyers. May our ignorance not lead us astray, success not deceive us, may our own interest or that of others not fail us. Bind us closely to you with the gift of your grace so that in you we may be one and never be distant from the truth. And since we are gathered together in your name, may justice guided by love govern us in all things, so that we may do nothing against your will in the present, and by our good acts earn eternal reward for the future.

Amen.

June 8, 1991

We thank you, Spirit of truth!
We thank you, Consoler,
because you brought us close to
the mystery of the pierced hands and feet,
the pierced side of God.
Because you have again brought us close to
the depth and the power
of the mystery of Redemption.

JUNE 10, 1990

Come Holy Spirit!
Come! Enter deep into the
hearts of those who belong to you.
May each be given
the manifestation of you
for the common good.
So that God may be all in all.
Amen.

JUNE 3, 1990

Lord,
give us a Spirit of faith
and knowledge,
give us a Spirit of kindness
and generosity,
give us a Spirit of love and unity.

JANUARY 25, 1993

The fruit of the Spirit is love,
patience, and generosity.
It is peace.

Send upon us, O Father,
a new effusion of the Spirit,
so that we may walk in a manner worthy
of the Christian vocation,
offering to the world the testimony
of the Gospels' truth
and inspiring the faithful
to unite all believers
in the chain of peace.

JANUARY 21, 1993

Spirit of eternal love,
who proceeds from the Father and the Son,
we thank you for all the vocations
of Apostles and Saints
which have enriched the Church.
We beg you to continue
this work of yours.
Remember when, at Pentecost,
you descended on the Apostles
gathered together in prayer
with Mary, the Mother of Jesus,
and look at your Church today, which has
a particular need for holy priests,
for faithful and authoritative witnesses
of your grace;
she needs consecrated men and women,
who demonstrate the joy
of those who live only for the Father,
who make their own the mission
and the offering of Christ,
who build up in charity
the new world.
Holy Spirit,
eternal spring of joy and peace,
it is you who open heart and mind
to the divine call;
you who make effective
every impulse to the good,
to truth, to charity.
Your sighs too deep for words

rise up to the Father from the heart of the Church,
which suffers and struggles for the Gospel.
Open the hearts and minds
of young men and women,
so that a new flowering
of holy vocations
may show forth the fidelity of your love,
and all may know Christ,
the true light coming into the world
to offer to every human being
the sure hope of eternal life.
Amen.

MESSAGE FOR THE WORLD DAY OF
PRAYER FOR VOCATIONS, 1998

Prayer for the second year of preparation for the Great Jubilee of 2000

Holy Spirit, sweetest guest of our hearts,
reveal to us the deep meaning
of the Great Jubilee
and impel our souls
to celebrate it with faith,
in the hope that doesn't disappoint,
in the charity that expects no return.
Spirit of truth,
who look into the depths of God,
who are the memory and prophecy of the Church,
lead humanity to recognize
in Jesus of Nazareth
the Lord of Glory,
the Savior of the world,
the supreme fulfillment of history.

Come, Spirit of love and peace!

Spirit Creator, mysterious maker of the Kingdom,
with the power of your holy gifts
guide the Church courageously
across the threshold
of the new millennium,
so she may bring to the generations to come
the light of the Word that saves.
Spirit of Holiness, divine breath

that moves the cosmos,
come, renew the face of the earth.
Rouse among Christians
the desire for total unity,
through being effective in the world
as the sign and instrument
of intimate union with God
and of the unity of all the human race.

Come, Spirit of love and peace!

Spirit of communion,
soul and foundation of the Church,
let the wealth of charisms and ministries
contribute to the unity of the Body of Christ;
let lay people, the consecrated, and ordained priests
agree to build together
the one and only Kingdom of God.
Spirit of consolation,
inexhaustible font of joy and peace,
inspire solidarity toward those who are in need,
provide comfort for the infirm,
instill trust and hope in those who are tested,
revive in everyone the commitment
to a better future.

Come, Spirit of love and peace!

Spirit of wisdom,
who touches minds and hearts,

direct the road
of science and technology
to serve life,
justice, and peace.
Make the dialogue
with those who belong to other religions productive,
make the different cultures open themselves
to the values of the Gospel.
Spirit of life, through whose action
the Word was made flesh
in the womb of the Virgin,
Our Lady who is silent and listening,
make us docile to the suggestions of your love,
and always ready to accept
the signs of the times
that you place on the roads of history.

Come, Spirit of love and peace!

To you, Spirit of love,
and to the Almighty Father
and the Only Begotten Son,
praise, honor, and glory
forever and ever world without end.
Amen.

To Mary

The Church sees the Blessed Mother of God . . .
present and sharing . . .
in the many complicated problems that today beset
the lives of individuals,
families, and nations.

Redemptoris Mater
(Encyclical, March 25, 1987)

See how plentiful the harvest is!

O Immaculate Virgin,
Mother of the true God and Mother of the Church!
You, who manifest your clemency
and your compassion for all those
who appeal to your protection,
hear the prayer that we address to you
with filial trust,
and present it to your Son Jesus,
our only Redeemer.

Mother of Mercy,
teacher of hidden, silent sacrifice,
to you, who come to meet us,
we sinners dedicate on this day
all our being
and all our love.
We dedicate to you also our life,
our work, our joys,
our weaknesses, and our sorrows.

Grant peace, justice, and prosperity
to our people,
since all that we have
and all that we are
we entrust to your care,
our Lady and Mother.

. . .

We wish to be completely yours
and travel with you on the road
of full faithfulness to Christ
in his Church:
hold us, always, tenderly by the hand.

Virgin Mother,
we pray to you for all the bishops,
may they guide the faithful
on the paths of a profoundly Christian life
of love and humble service
to God and our souls.
See how plentiful the harvest is,
and intercede with the Lord
so that he may instill a hunger for holiness
in all the people of God
and grant abundant vocations
of priests and religious, strong in the faith
and eager dispensers of the mysteries of God.

Grant our families
the grace to love
and respect life that is beginning,
with the same love with which
you conceived the life of the Son of God
in your womb.

Virgin Holy Mary, Mother of beautiful love,
protect our families,
so that they may always stay together,

and bless the education of our children.
Our hope,
look on us with pity,
teach us to go continually to Jesus,
and if we fall, help us to raise ourselves,
to return to him,
through the confession
of our sins
in the Sacrament of Repentance,
which brings tranquillity to our souls.
We beg you to grant us
a great love
for all the Sacraments,
which are the signs that your Son
left us on earth.
Thus, Most Holy Mary,
with God's peace in our consciousness,
with our hearts free
from malice and hatred,
we will be able to bring to all true joy
and true peace,
which come to us from your Son,
our Lord Jesus Christ,
who with the Father and the Holy Spirit
lives and reigns forever and ever.
Amen.

1979

With Rome, with the Church, with the world

Hail!

We come together today to greet you, Mary, who were chosen to be the Mother of the Eternal Word.

Hail! *Blessed art thou, O full of grace.*

We use the words uttered by Gabriel, the messenger of the Most Holy Trinity.

We use these words uttered by all the generations of the people of God who in the space of nearly two thousand years have already completed their pilgrimage on this earth. We use these words, dictated by our hearts: *"Ave Maria, gratia plena": full of grace.* We gather today, the day when the Church, with deep veneration, recalls the full measure of this grace, which God filled you with from the very moment of your conception.

The words of the Apostle bring us great joy: "Where sin increased, grace abounded all the more."

We are happy with this special abundance in you of divine grace, which bears the name of "Immaculate Conception."

Accept us, just as we are, here beside you.

Accept us! Look into our hearts! Accept our worries and our hopes!

Help us, you who are full of grace, to live in grace, to persevere in grace, and, if necessary, return to the grace of the living God, who is the greatest and supernatural good of man.

Prepare us for the coming of your Son!

Accept us, with our daily problems, our weaknesses and shortcomings, our crises and our personal, family, and social failings.

Do not allow us to lose our good will. Help us to be always sincere in our conscience and honest in our conduct.

With your prayers, obtain justice for us. Preserve peace throughout the world!

In a short while we will all depart from this place. Yet we hope to return to our houses with the joyous certainty that you are with us, you, Immaculate One, chosen from the beginning of time to be the Mother of the Redeemer. You are with us. You are with the Church and with the world. Amen.

DECEMBER 8, 1979

Mother of Beautiful Love!

Hail, O Mother, Queen of the world.
You are the Mother of beautiful love,
you are the Mother of Jesus
the source of all grace,
the perfume of every virtue,
the mirror of all purity.
You are joy in distress,
victory in battle,
hope in death.
How sweet the taste
of your name on our lips,
how gentle the harmony
in our ears,
what ecstasy in our hearts!
You are happiness for those who suffer,
the crown of martyrs
the beauty of virgins.
We implore you that after this exile
you will lead us
to possess your Son, Jesus.
Amen.

Look at us favorably

O Most Holy Virgin, Mother of God, Mother of Christ, Mother of the Church, look at us favorably in this hour!

Virgo fidelis, faithful Virgin, pray for us! Teach us to believe as you believed! Let our faith in God, in Christ, in the Church be always pure, serene, courageous, strong, generous.

Mater amabilis, Mother worthy of love! *Mater pulchrae dilectionis,* Mother of beautiful love, pray for us. Teach us to love God and our brothers, as you loved them: let our love for others be always patient, kind, respectful.

Causa nostrae laetitiae, cause of our joy, pray for us! Teach us how to grasp, in faith, the paradox of Christian joy, which originates and flourishes in pain, in renunciation, in union with your crucified Son: may our joy be always authentic and full, so that it can be communicated to all!

Amen!

May 31, 1979

Mother of God and men

Our Lady and Mother! At the beginning of the story of salvation, the Eternal Father made his resolve and chose you, Immaculate One, to be the Mother of the Word made flesh. And at the beginning of the struggle between good and evil he chose you, as the woman who *crushes the head of the serpent.* In this way he marked your humble maternity as the sign of hope for all those who, in this battle, in this struggle, wish to persevere with your Son and vanquish evil with good.

As we approach the end of the second millennium, we feel these struggles profoundly. The events around us show us continually how threatening are the forces of sin, hatred, brutality, and death. So again we look to the Mother of the Redeemer of the world, to the Lady of the Apocalypse of John, to the "woman clothed with the sun" in whom we see you, welling up with light, which illuminates the dark and perilous stages of human life on earth.

O Mother, let this prayer and this abandon, which we renew yet again, tell you everything about us. Bring us close to you, again, Mother of God and men—Comforter, Protector, great Mother of God and our mother, and *come to us again.* Do not let the brothers and sisters of your Son perish. Give our hearts the power of truth. Give peace and order to our existence.

Show yourself a mother!
Queen of Heaven, rejoice!

TURIN, APRIL 13, 1980

"O Mary, conceived without sin, pray for us who have recourse to thee." This is the prayer that you, O Mary, inspired in St. Catherine Labouré; and this invocation, now stamped on the medal, is spoken by many of the faithful throughout the world who wear this medal.

Today the Church celebrates the visit that you made to Elizabeth when the Son of God had become flesh in your womb; and our first prayer is to praise you and bless you. You are blessed among women. Blessed are you who believed! The Almighty has made miracles through you. The miracle of your divine Maternity! And, in expectation of that, the miracle of your Immaculate Conception. The miracle of your "yes."

You were so intimately joined to the work of our Redemption, to the Cross of our Savior, that your heart was pierced by it, beside his heart.

And now, in the glory of your Son, you continue to intercede for us, poor sinners. You, the Mother of the Church, watch over her. You watch over each of your children. You obtain for us from God all the graces symbolized by the rays of light radiating from your open hands. On the sole condition that we dare to ask them from you, that we approach you with the trust, the boldness, the simplicity of a child. Thus you always lead us toward your divine Son.

Today, in this holy place, I also wish to reiterate to you the trust, the deep attachment that you have always shown me: "*Totus tuus:* entirely yours."

We dedicate to you our power and our willingness to serve the design of salvation brought about by your Son.

We pray to you that, thanks to the Holy Spirit, faith may deepen and be affirmed in all Christians, and that hope may be revived in all those who lose heart.

We pray to you in particular for this people, for the Church, for its pastors, for the consecrated, for the fathers and mothers of families, for children and young people, for men and women in their old age.

We pray to you for those who suffer because of some physical or moral affliction, or who are tempted to be unfaithful, or are shaken by doubt in a climate of disbelief, for those who endure persecution because of their faith.

We entrust to you the Apostolate of lay people, the ministry of priests, the testimony of religious.

We pray to you that the vocation to the priestly and religious life may be widely understood and followed, for the glory of God and for the vitality of the Church in this nation and in the nations that are waiting for missionary cooperation.

PARIS, MAY 31, 1980

Mary, star of evangelization

Mary, under the inspiration of the Holy Spirit, you said that the generations would call you blessed. We take up the hymn of past generations, so that it is not interrupted, and we exalt in you that which is most luminous, and which humanity offered to God: the human creature in its perfection, newly created in justice and holiness, in an incomparable beauty that we call "Immaculate" or "full of grace."

Mother, you are the "new Eve." The Church of your Son is aware that only with "new men" can there be evangelization, that is, can the Good News be brought to the world, so that, through your intercession, the newness of the Gospel—the seed of holiness and fruitfulness—is never absent from her.

Mary, we adore the Father for the qualities that shine in you, but we adore him also because for us you are always "the Handmaiden of the Lord," little creature. Because you were able to say, *"fiat"*—"let it be"—you became the Bride of the Holy Spirit and the Mother of the Son of God.

Mother, who appears in the pages of the Gospel showing Christ to the shepherds and the wise men, let every evangelizer—bishop, priest, religious, nun, father or mother, youth or child—be possessed by Christ so that he can reveal him to others.

Mary, who are hidden in the crowd while your Son performs the miraculous signs of the coming of the Kingdom of God, and who speak only to say that you will do all that he asks, help the evangelizers preach not themselves but Jesus Christ.

Mother, shrouded in the mystery of your Son, often without understanding, yet taking in everything and pondering in your heart, make us evangelizers aware that, beyond technology and strategy, preparations and plans, to evangelize is to immerse ourselves in the mystery of Christ and attempt to communicate something of him to our brothers and sisters.

Madonna of humility in truth, who taught us in the prophetic canticle that "God always exalts the humble," help "the simple and the poor," who seek you with popular piety, help the pastors guide them to the light of truth, and, when the pastors must eradicate elements that are no longer genuine and purify expressions of popular devotion, let them be strong and understanding at the same time.

Mother, like the Disciples at the Last Supper, we ask for your intercession, for the constant assistance of the Holy Spirit and the docility to welcome him in the Church; we ask for those who seek the truth of God and for those who must serve it and live it. May Christ forever be the "light of the world" and may the world recognize us as his disciples so that we may abide in his word and know the truth that will make us free with the freedom of children of God. So let it be.

JULY 8, 1980

Loving Comforter

O Most Holy Virgin, may you be the only and everlasting consolation of the Church whom you love and protect! Comfort your bishops and your priests, missionaries and religious, who must enlighten and save modern society, which is difficult and sometimes hostile. Comfort the Christian communities, by giving them the gift of many strong priestly and religious vocations!

Comfort all those who are charged with civil and religious, social and political authority and responsibility, so that they may have as their single, constant goal the common good and integral development of humanity, in spite of difficulties and defeats.

Comfort this people, which loves you and worships you; comfort the many immigrant families, the unemployed, the suffering, those who carry in body and soul the wounds caused by extreme situations; comfort the young, especially those who find themselves for so many painful reasons confused and discouraged; comfort those who feel in their hearts yearning for altruistic love, for charity, for self-giving, all those who cultivate high ideals of spiritual and social accomplishment.

O Mother and Comforter, comfort us all, and make all understand that the secret of happiness lies in goodness, and in faithfully following your son, Jesus.

April 14, 1980

O Virgin, morning star,

the hope and dawn of salvation for the entire world, turn your kind maternal gaze upon us who are gathered here to celebrate and proclaim your glories.

O Virgin most faithful,

who have always been ready and eager to welcome, guard, and meditate on the Word of God, grant that we, too, amid the dramatic events of history, may be able to maintain our Christian faith intact, the precious treasure handed down to us by our fathers!

O Virgin most powerful,

who with your foot crush the head of the serpent that tempts us, grant that we may fulfill, day after day, our baptismal promises, to renounce Satan, his works and his seductions, and enable us to give to the world joyous testimony of Christian hope.

O Virgin most merciful,

who have always opened your Mother's heart to the invocations of humanity, sometimes divided by dislike and also, unfortunately, by hatred and war, grant that, following the teaching of your Son, we may all grow in unity and peace, to become worthy sons of the one heavenly Father.

Amen!

SEPTEMBER 8, 1980

To your care I entrust...

Hail Mary, Mother of Christ and of the Church! Hail, our sweetest life and hope.

To your care I entrust the needs of all families, the joys of children, the desires of young people, the anxieties of adults, the pain of the sick, and a serene old age for the elderly.

To you I entrust the faithfulness and self-denial of the ministers of your Son, the hope of those who are preparing for this ministry, the joyous self-giving of cloistered virgins, the prayer and concern of men and women religious, the life and commitment of all those who work for the Kingdom of Christ on this earth.

In your hands I place the sweat and labor of those who work with their hands; the noble dedication of those who transmit their knowledge and the efforts of those who learn; the great vocation of those who through science and service alleviate the pain of others; the work of those who with their intelligence seek the truth.

In your heart I leave the goals of those who honestly seek and strive for the economic prosperity of their brothers and sisters; of those who, in the service of truth, inform and form public opinion; of those who, in politics, in the army, in the unions, or in the police, lend their honest cooperation to insure that we live together in justice, peace, and security.

Holy Virgin, increase our faith, fortify our hope, revive our charity.

Succor those who suffer misfortunes, those who suffer solitude, ignorance, or hunger or unemployment. Strengthen those whose faith is weak.

Arouse in young people the willingness to give themselves totally to God.

And bring a mother's help, O Mary, to those who invoke you as their Benefactress.

So let it be.

NOVEMBER 6, 1982

We have recourse to your protection, Holy Mother of God

"We have recourse to your protection, Holy Mother of God!"

Mother of individuals and peoples, you who "know all their sufferings and their hopes." You who have a mother's awareness of all the struggles between good and evil, between light and darkness, which afflict the modern world, hear our cry that, as if moved by the Holy Spirit, we address directly to your heart. Embrace, with the love of the Mother and the Handmaiden, this human world of ours, which we entrust and consecrate to you, for we are filled with concern for the earthly and eternal destiny of individuals and peoples.

In a special way we entrust and consecrate to you those individuals and *those nations* that particularly need to be entrusted and consecrated.

"We have recourse to your protection, Holy Mother of God!"

Do not reject the prayers that we who are in need send up to you!

Do not reject us!

Accept our humble trust—and our act of entrusting!

Before you, Mother of Christ, before your Immaculate heart, I today, together with the whole Church, unite myself with our Redeemer in this his consecration for the world and for people, which only in his divine heart has the power to obtain pardon and to secure reparation.

Above all may you be blessed, you, the Handmaiden of the Lord, who in the fullest way obey the divine call!

Hail to you, who *are wholly united* to the redeeming consecration of your Son!

Mother of the Church! Enlighten the people of God along the paths of faith, hope, and charity. Help us to live with the whole truth of the consecration of Christ, for the entire human family in the modern world.

In entrusting to you, O Mother, the world, all individuals and all peoples, *we also entrust to you the consecration itself,* for the world's sake, placing it in your motherly heart.

Oh, Immaculate Heart! Help us to vanquish the threat of evil, which so easily takes root in the hearts of the people of today, and whose immeasurable effects already weigh down on our modern world and seem to block the paths to the future!

From hunger and war, *deliver us!*

From nuclear war, from incalculable self-destruction, from every kind of war, *deliver us!*

From sins against the life of man from its very beginning, *deliver us!*

From hatred and from the demeaning of the dignity of the children of God, *deliver us!*

From every kind of injustice in the life of society, national, and international, *deliver us!*

From readiness to trample the commandments of God, *deliver us!*

From attempts to stifle in human hearts the very truth of God, *deliver us!*

From sins against the Holy Spirit, *deliver us! Deliver us!*

Accept, O Mother of Christ, this cry laden with the sufferings of all individuals, *laden with the sufferings* of whole societies!

May the infinite power of your *merciful love* be revealed yet again in the history of the world. May it stop evil! May it transform consciences! May your Immaculate Heart reveal for all the *light of hope!*

ACT OF CONSECRATION TO MARY, FATIMA,
MAY 13, 1982

Be the light of the new Coming!

Immaculate One! Mother of God and men!

We come to you to worship the marvelous work that the Most Holy Trinity has accomplished in you, in the birth of Christ, the Redeemer of the world and your Son: we thank God for you, first among the redeemed; for you, who—among all the children of Adam—were saved from original sin.

O Mary! *Be the Mother of our deliverance from every evil:* from the evil that oppresses men's conscience, and from the even more threatening evil that darkens the horizon of our century.

You are the light of the first *Coming!* You are the morning star that precedes the advent of the Messiah. Now that the Church and humanity approach the end of the *second millennium* after the Coming of Christ—be for us the light of this new Coming, be the morning star, so that we are not shrouded in darkness!

O Mary, intervene and, with your gentle Mother's voice, speak to the heart of those who decide the destinies of peoples, so that through dialogue they may find the way to fair and honorable settlements of the conflicts that divide them. Persuade men in arms in the various parts of the world to hear the cry for peace that comes to them from martyred and defenseless populations.

O Mary, revive in the hearts of all individuals a feeling of human solidarity toward those who, without food, are dying of hunger; who, fleeing their homelands, seek refuge for themselves and their families; who, left without work, see their future dangerously threatened.

O Mary, protect the innocent purity in the children of today, who will be the adults of the millennial future. Your Immaculate Conception reflects with dazzling brightness the light that descended into the world: the Lord Christ. Let this *light lead us toward the future!* Be with us now, forever and in the *hour of our death.* Amen.

DECEMBER 8, 1983

Mary, teach us love

O Mary, full of grace, immaculate, the forever virgin Mother of Christ, the Mother of God and our mother, assumed into Heaven, Blessed Queen, model of the Church and our hope, we offer our humble filial wish to honor you and celebrate you always with a special reverence that recognizes the marvels God wrought in you, with a special devotion that expresses our most pious, most pure, most human, most personal, most confidential feelings, and insures that the beautiful example of human perfection shines forth high above the world.

O Mary, we pray to you: let us understand, desire, possess in tranquillity purity of body and soul.

Teach us meditation and interiority; make us open to good inspirations and the Word of God; teach us the need for contemplation, for a personal inner life, for the private prayer that God alone sees.

Mary, teach us love. We ask you for love, Mary, love for Christ, the only love, the highest love, total love, giving love, love in sacrifice for our brothers and sisters. Help us to love in this way.

Obtain for us, O Mary, faith, supernatural faith, simple faith, full and strong, sincere faith, derived from its true source, the Word of God, and from its flawless conduit, the Magisterium established and guaranteed by Christ, the living faith!

O Mary, "blessed because you believed," comfort us with your example, obtain for us this charism.

And further, O Mary, we ask that your example and your intercession may bring us hope. We greet our hope! We are in need of hope, desperately in need of hope!

You, Mary, are the image and the beginning of the Church; you shine forth now before the people of God as a sure sign of hope and consolation, O Mary, Mother of the Church.

PRAYER OF PAUL VI, REPEATED BY
JOHN PAUL II, NOVEMBER 2, 1984

Mary is the star who lights the way

Mary, star of the sea! We come to you today, placing at your feet the evils that oppress us, certain of finding in your Mother's heart understanding and forgiveness, encouragement and comfort. We entrust to you, O Mary, our joys and our sorrows, our expectations and disappointments, our desires, plans, hopes. Accept the resolutions of purity, altruism, cooperation that we keep in our hearts, and obtain for our fragile wills the gift of courage and perseverance.

We entrust to you, O Mother, families, the fundamental units of the Church and the primordial cells in which the faith of new Christian generations develops. Protect them from the many temptations to which the modern world exposes them, and which are often so alien to the values of the Gospel, and help them to fulfill in the affairs of daily life the marvelous design that God has drawn for them from "the beginning."

We entrust to you, Mother of individuals and peoples, the communities and the parishes. Let them be witnesses to the faith, living the communion of charity, in a spirit of mutual respect and constructive cooperation.

We entrust to you, finally, the Church, which in the course of centuries has made present in this nation the mystery of the Word Incarnate, who died and rose for the salvation of mankind. Spread your mantle over her and protect her from every danger. Star of the sea, be a sure guide for her always, so that, in the harmony of Catholic communion, she may make a tranquil journey to the longed-for port of Heaven.

Amen.

MAY 14, 1985

O Mother, spread your mantle over all of us

Blessed Virgin Mary, your birth fills us all with great joy. In you shines the dawn of redemption, because you gave birth to Christ for us, the sun of justice. As the Mother of the Savior of the world, and as the Mother of the Church, you help us meet the Christ in our life. You, the Virgin forever pure and spotless, guide us on the sure way and lead us out of the shadows of sin and death to the divine light of your Son, who in the Holy Spirit has reconciled us with the Heavenly Father and, through the service of the Church, continues to reconcile us with him.

Holy Mother of God! Confidently I entrust to you families and communities, the authorities of the Church, of the state, and of society, children and young people, the sick and the old, the dead, who in their tombs await the Resurrection. To your powerful intercession I entrust all the people of God, and declare that you are the *Mater fortior* for us all.

Yes, Mother most powerful! You, Mother of God, are stronger than all the forces hostile to God, which threaten our world and our nation. You are stronger than the temptations and assaults that would sever man from God and his Commandments. You are stronger than every selfish and personal ambition that obscures our vision of God and our neighbor. You are stronger, because you believed, you hoped, and you loved fully. You are stronger, because you fulfilled the will of God completely and followed the path of your Son, obedient and faithful, to the Cross. You are stronger, because you share body and soul in the Paschal victory of the

Lord. Truly, you are stronger, because the Almighty has accomplished great things in you.

Fervently I pray to you: "Virgin, Mother of my God, make me all yours! Yours in life, yours in death, yours in suffering, fear, and misery; yours on the Cross and in painful affliction. Yours in time and in eternity. Virgin, Mother of my God, make me entirely yours!" Amen.

ACT OF CONSECRATION TO MARY,
SEPTEMBER 8, 1985

We turn to you with the trust of children

Mary, star of the sea, God the Father has infused you with the Holy Spirit, so that, becoming the Mother of Jesus, you would become our Mother, too.

We turn to you with the trust of children: you who know the physical and spiritual dangers and difficulties that threaten seafaring people, protect all sailors and the families that wait for them.

You who are the Gate of Heaven and the Comforter of the afflicted, intercede so that those who are lost at sea, who lie under your maternal gaze, may enter into the glory of paradise; comfort the families that grieve for them.

Support the priests and lay people who, among the people of the sea, are committed to bring the Word and the witness of the Gospel.

Give us all the desire and the strength to live as true disciples of your Son who lives and reigns forever and ever.

JUNE 17, 1985

Guide us on our way

We turn to you, Holy Immaculate Virgin. In you begins the mystery of Redemption, which frees us from death, because you did not receive the inheritance of sin. You are full of grace, and in you the Kingdom of God opens to us, the new future of mankind, which can, in faith, contemplate in you the action of renewal and the foundation of the hope of immortality. You bring us, in your purity, the Son of God, the "light that came into the world," and lead us along the paths of holiness so that we may meet Christ, now and forever.

We beseech you, guide us on our way, Holy Virgin, so that by making active the truth we may reach the light of your Son, seek the grace of his Word, travel faithfully the road that leads to the mountain of God, to the gentle harbor that our dear ones have reached, and where, with Jesus, you wait for us.

Amen.

NOVEMBER 2, 1986

We consecrate ourselves to you

Hail Mary!
With the angel we greet you: full of grace.
The Lord is with you.
We greet you with Elizabeth. You are blessed among women, and blessed is the fruit of your womb; blessed are you, because you believed in the divine promises!
We greet you with the words of the Gospel:
You are blessed because you listened to the Word of God and fulfilled it.

You are full of grace!
We praise you, beloved daughter of the Father.
We bless you, Mother of the divine Word.
We worship you, house of the Holy Spirit.
We call on you, Mother and model of the whole Church.
We contemplate you, the perfect image of the hopes of all humanity.

The Lord is with you!
You are the Virgin of the Annunciation, the "yes" of all humanity to the mystery of salvation.
You are the Daughter of Zion and the Ark of the New Covenant in the mystery of the Visitation.
You are the Mother of Jesus who was born in Bethlehem, she who showed him to the simple shepherds and to the wise men of the east.

You are the Mother who presents her Son in the temple, accompanies him into Egypt, leads him into Nazareth.
Virgin of the paths of Jesus, of the hidden life and of the miracle at Cana.
Grieving Mother of Calvary and glorious Virgin of the Resurrection.
You are the Mother of the Disciples of Jesus in the expectation and joy of Pentecost.

Blessed . . .
because you believed in the Word of the Lord
because you placed hope in his promises
because you were perfect in love
because of your attentive charity toward Elizabeth
for your maternal kindness in Bethlehem
for your strength in persecution,
for your perseverance in the search for Jesus in the temple,
for your simple life in Nazareth,
for your intercession in Cana,
for your maternal presence at the foot of the Cross,
for your faith in the expectation of Resurrection,
for your constant prayer at Pentecost.
You are blessed for the glory of your Assumption into Heaven
for your maternal protection of the Church
for your constant intercession for all mankind.

Holy Mary, Mother of God!
We wish to consecrate ourselves to you.
Because you are the Mother of God and our mother.
Because your Son Jesus entrusted us to you.

To you I consecrate the entire Church, with its pastors and its faithful.
The bishops, who in imitation of the Good Shepherd watch over the people who have been entrusted to them.
The priests, who have been anointed by the Spirit.
Men and women religious, who offer their lives to the Kingdom of Christ.
Seminarians, who have accepted the call of the Lord.
Christian husbands and wives, in the unity and indissolubility of their love and their families.
Lay people engaged in the Apostolate.
Young people who yearn for a new society.
Children, who deserve a more humane and peaceful world.
The sick, the poor, the incarcerated, the persecuted, orphans, the desperate, and those about to die.
To you I consecrate the entire nation, of which you are the Patroness and Queen.
May the values of the Gospel shine in its institutions.

Pray for us sinners!
Mother of the Church, we have recourse to your protection and we entrust ourselves to your inspiration.

We ask that the Church may be faithful in the purity of faith, in the steadfastness of hope, in the ardor of charity, in apostolic and missionary generosity, in the commitment to promote justice and peace among the children of this blessed earth.

We entreat you for the whole Church: that she may remain forever in the perfect communion of faith and love, united to the See of Peter by tight bonds of obedience and charity.

We pray to you for success in the new evangelization, for fidelity to preferential love for the poor and to the Christian formation of young people, for an increase in priestly and religious vocations, for generosity in those who devote themselves to the mission, to unity, and to the sanctity of families.

Now and in the hour of our death!
Virgin of the Rosary, our Mother! Pray for us now.

Grant us the precious gift of peace.

Of forgiving all hatred and bitterness, and reconciling all our brothers and sisters.

May violence and warfare cease.

May dialogue progress and take root, and peaceful coexistence begin.

May new pathways of justice and prosperity be opened up. We ask this of you whom we invoke as the Queen of Peace. Now and in the hour of our death!

We entrust to you all the victims of injustice and violence, all those who have died in natural catastrophes, all those who in the hour of death turn to you as Mother and Patroness.

Be for all of us, Gate of Heaven, life, sweetness, and hope, so that together with you we may glorify the Father, the Son, and the Holy Spirit.

Amen!

JULY 3, 1986

Queen of Peace

Holy Virgin,
you who lived in faith
the difficult moments of family life,
secure peace for nations at war
and help the families of the world
to carry out their indispensable
mission of peace.

DECEMBER 12, 1993

Give us peace and unity

Holy Mother of God,
you who are vaster than Heaven,
since you contained in yourself
he whom Heaven cannot contain,
turn your maternal gaze toward this house
where men and women seek,
in the silence of listening
and in the communion of hearts,
a future of faith for Europe
where they strive to discover
what the hands of the men and women
of today, reaching out, wish to grasp.
Give them the peace of pilgrims
and the joy of walking together,
so that Europe, too,
may welcome more and more to its bosom,
as you welcomed
the Word of life,
the only hope of the world.

DECEMBER 12, 1993

We appeal to your maternal love

Mother of the Redeemer and our Mother,
trustfully we appeal to your maternal love and ask for your help.
In the present pass of civilization
grant all the sons and daughters of the Church
the courage to live profoundly
the message of your divine Son,
"Way, Truth, and Life,"
by rediscovering the wealth of their great traditions.
May they translate it into works,
so that it will be an active yeast of spirituality and humanity,
in every layer of the fabric of society:
in the family, the school, the world of work and culture,
in the places where the fates of communities are decided.
Queen of Heaven and our hope,
I place in your maternal heart
the problems and the anxieties, the yearnings and the hopes
of these beloved populations, who have confidence in you.
I entrust to your Immaculate heart all the people of God—
priests, men and women religious and lay faithful—
so that in all of them there may be
a livelier awareness that they must be bold witnesses
to the values proclaimed by the Gospel,
in the face of the afflictions of daily life.
With very special emphasis, I entrust to you,
to your tender and open heart,
young people and their high ideals.
They will be the ones who, in the year 2000,

will bear witness to the vitality of today and will gather—
God willing!—the fruits.
May they now be among those who fashion the good things,
peace and hope above all,
which the modern world has in great part lost
and is anxiously seeking.
Amen.

May 24, 1987

Sustain us on the path of faith

Mother of the Redeemer,
joyfully we proclaim that you are blessed.
Before the world was created,
God the Father chose you
to fulfill his providential
plan of salvation.
You believed in his love
and obeyed his word.
The Son of God wanted you for his Mother,
when he became man to save man.
You received him
with eager obedience
and an undivided heart.
The Holy Spirit loved you
as his mystical spouse
and filled you with wonderful gifts.
Docilely you let yourself be molded
by his powerful hidden action.

On the eve of the third Christian millennium,
we entrust the Church to you,
she recognizes you and invokes you as her Mother.
You, who preceded her on earth
in the pilgrimage of faith,
comfort her in trials and tribulations,
and grant that she may be
an ever more effective

sign and instrument in the world
of the intimate union with God
and of the unity of the whole human race.

To you, Mother of individuals and nations,
we confidently entrust all humanity
with its hopes and fears.
Do not let the light
of true wisdom fail.
Guide us in the search for liberty
and justice for all.
Direct our steps along the paths of peace.
Let us all encounter Christ,
the way, the truth, and the life.
O Virgin Mary, sustain
us on the road of faith
and obtain for us the grace of eternal salvation.
O clement, O pious, O sweet Mother of God
and our Mother, Mary!

PRAYER FOR THE START OF
THE MARIAN YEAR,
JUNE 6, 1987

To you, O Mother, I entrust the Christian people

I lift up my eyes to you, O Virgin of Sorrows. To you, who remind us how high the price of our Redemption was, I entrust this beloved Church. You protect her. You strengthen her. You guide her on the pilgrimage of faith!

To you I entrust the pastor, and the priests and the deacons who collaborate with him in the various ecclesial ministries, the people who have consecrated their lives entirely to your Son and those who are inwardly called to a similar gesture of giving.

I commend to you young people, the springtime of the Church and society: do not let the hurricane of passion or the chill of depression destroy the flowering of enthusiasm in them and, with it, the promise of fruits.

In your hands, O Virgin, I place the hopes and disappointments, the joys and sorrows of the families whom love, strengthened by the Sacrament, has generated on this earth, which is dear to you: protect husbands and wives from everything that threatens the firmness of their mutual commitment; help children open themselves trustfully to the educational work of those who have given them life; comfort old people and the sick with the understanding and support of one who is still young and vigorous.

I entrust to you, O Mother, all Christian people, who live, struggle, suffer, and love on this earth; may their faith remain *solid* as rock; *pure* as the water of a mountain stream; *fruitful* with good works as the fertile valleys.

Welcome under your mantle this chosen portion of your Son's flock and lead it on sure paths to the fields of eternal life, O clement, O pious, O sweet Virgin Mary!

APRIL 17, 1988

The prayer of lay people to Mary

O Most Blessed Virgin Mary,
Mother of Christ and Mother of the Church,
with joy and wonder
we seek to make our own your Magnificat,
joining you in your hymn of thankfulness and
love.

With you we give thanks to God,
"whose mercy
is from generation to generation,"
for the exalted vocation
and the many forms of mission
entrusted to the lay faithful.
God has called each of them by name
to live his own communion of love
and holiness
and to be one
in the great family of God's children.
He has sent them forth
to shine with the light of Christ
and to communicate the fire of the Spirit
in every part of society
through their life
inspired by the Gospel.

. . .

O Virgin of the Magnificat,
fill their hearts
with gratitude and enthusiasm
for this vocation and mission.
With humility and magnanimity
you were the Handmaiden of the Lord;
give us your unreserved willingness
for service to God
and the salvation of the world.
Open our hearts
to the great anticipation
of the Kingdom of God
and of the proclamation of the Gospel
to the whole of Creation.
Your Mother's heart
is ever mindful of the many dangers
and evils that threaten
to overpower men and women
in our time.
But your heart also takes notice
of the many initiatives
undertaken for good,
the great yearning for values,
and the progress achieved
in bringing forth
the abundant fruits of salvation.
O Virgin full of courage,
may your spiritual strength
and trust in God inspire us,

so that we may know
how to overcome all the obstacles
that we encounter
in accomplishing our mission.
Teach us to treat the affairs
of the world
with a real sense of Christian responsibility
and a joyful hope
of the coming of God's Kingdom, and
of a new Heaven and a new earth.

You who were gathered in prayer
with the Apostles in the upper rooms,
awaiting the coming
of the Spirit at Pentecost,
implore his renewed outpouring
on all the faithful, men and women alike,
so that they may more fully respond
to their vocation and mission,
as branches engrafted to the true vine,
called to bear much fruit
for the life of the world.

O Virgin Mother,
guide and sustain us
so that we may always live
as true sons and daughters
of the Church of your Son.
Enable us to do our part

in helping to establish on earth
the civilization of truth and love,
as God wills it,
for his glory.
Amen.

Christifideles Laici
(Apostolic Exhortation,
December 30, 1988)

Mother of the risen Christ

O Mother of the Redeemer, who was crucified and is risen, Mother who became ours at the moment when Christ, by dying, performed the supreme act of his love for men, help us! Pray for us! We need to live, with you, as the risen. We must, and we will, let go of every demeaning compromise with sin; we must, and we will, walk with you, following Christ. *"Succurre cadenti surgere qui curat populo." (Assist your people who have fallen yet strive to rise again.)* Today we join the ancient Antiphon of Advent with the Antiphon of Easter: *"Resurrexit sicut dixit, alleluia! Ora pro nobis, Deum, alleluia." (He has risen as he said, alleluia. Pray for us, Lord, alleluia.)*

Your Son is risen; your Son prays for us. We, too, are risen with him; we, too, wish to live as the risen. Sustain us in this "unending challenge to human awareness . . . the challenge to follow, by both old means and new, the path of 'not falling,' which is the path of 'rising.' "

Ora pro nobis Deum! As we approach the third Christian millennium, pray for us, Lord! Deliver us from evil; from war, hatred, hypocrisy, mutual misunderstanding; from hedonism, impurity, selfishness, hardheartedness. Deliver us!

Ora pro nobis Deum! Alleluia.

APRIL 6, 1988

Mary and the Eucharist

Hail Mary, full of grace, Mother of mercy! We render thanks to you because you gave us the blessed fruit of your womb, Jesus Christ, the author of our salvation.

You, the Mother and guardian of this people, accompanied it through history, its teacher in faith, hope, and life: now show us Jesus, offering us the example of his life and interceding for us.

In this hour of grace and benediction, we wish to reaffirm our faith in Christ Eucharist, the Way, the Truth, and the Life: we wish to welcome his Word into our hearts, just as you did, so that renewed by the Eucharist and the Word we may all together build the longed-for civilization of love.

Our Lady of Evangelization! Mother of the Good News, we know that the road is arduous; this glorious earth, the cradle of Saints, is now afflicted by violence and death, by poverty and injustice, by a profound crisis in the family caused by neglect of the law of the Lord, by ideologies that seek to empty the earth of its Christian faith.

For this reason we wish to offer you all the people of God, and place them near your maternal heart:

–The pastors of the Church, so that they may continue to be firm teachers of the truth, defenders of the dignity of their brothers and sisters, builders of unity.

–The priests, so that, with increased awareness of their bond with the sole Mediator, Jesus Christ, they may fortify their presence in the community, as faithful dispensers of the mysteries of God.

–The consecrated, so that by faithful observance of the evangelical counsels they may give themselves intensely to God as to their supreme love; may they be a luminous sign of the Church and the presence of your Son in the world.

–All lay people, so that, faithful to their baptism and guided by the Holy Spirit, they may become authentic witnesses to the Gospel and announce it with their lives.

–Christian families, so that, as true domestic churches, they may be authentic sanctuaries where faith, hope, and charity live, where faithfulness, filial obedience, and mutual love flourish.

–Young people, so that they may devote all their energy to building up a new nation in which the spirit of the beatitudes of the Kingdom can live without fear.

–The poor, the old, the sick, the victims of injustice and violence, those who carry the Cross of the Passion of your Son, so that they may find comfort in their faith, strength in their hope, a firm source of aid in all their brothers.

–The leaders of governments and those who rule society, so that righteously and with generous commitment they may lead their people on the paths of justice and freedom to peaceful coexistence.

Our Mother and Our Lady, lovingly welcome this offering of your children and bless this beloved land with the gifts of reconciliation and peace.

O clement, O pious, O sweet Virgin Mary!

May 14, 1988

Virgin most prudent

Hail, Virgin most prudent,
Mother of Christ and our Mother, Mary.
Blessed are you,
who have journeyed on the roads of the earth
with a heart attentive to the God of the Covenant,
and a watchful eye on the needs of our brothers and sisters.
Intercede for us with your Son Jesus
and obtain for us the gift
of prudence in driving,
respect for the law of the road,
generous attention to our traveling companions.
With maternal love watch over your children
who walk on the streets of the world,
so that their journey may be smooth,
their travels rich in experiences of humanity,
their return happy.
Virgin,
shining star and constant guide,
illumine our path
and make the road of life secure,
so that we may arrive at the
ultimate and definitive encounter
with Christ, your Son and our Lord.
He lives and reigns forever and ever.
Amen.

SEPTEMBER 17, 1989

Hail, Mother of the Redeemer,
luminous icon of the Church,
our Mother and sister
on the path of faith.

From east to west,
with one voice, we raise with you
the song of praise
to the one and only Lord.

Through you hope is reborn
beyond the millennium that is closing,
to the new one that approaches.

Merciful one, pray for us:
the Spirit of your Son,
wisdom of the heart
days of peace.

AUGUST 15, 1990

O Virgin full of grace

O Virgin full of grace, teach young people the duty of molding their hearts in the school of the divine Teacher, your Son Jesus. Give those who are called to the priesthood a longing for true greatness, a desire for evangelical perfection, a passion for the salvation of souls, the courage and generosity to follow Christ wherever he goes. Support the future workers in the harvest on every step of their way to the altar, in every choice connected with true ecclesial service, every sacrifice necessary to be faithful to Christ with an undivided heart.

Let the new presbyters be able to understand the "secrets" of God, of readily welcoming the petitions of men, of responding to their problems, and especially those of the poorest and lowliest, imitating the generous dedication of your Son Jesus. Grant that in prayer, in the Eucharist, in meditation on the revealed Word they may find the strength to be more holy every day.

July 2, 1990

Help us reach the horizons of hope

Glorious and Blessed Virgin,
great Mother of God, Most Holy Mary,
look upon this diocesan community,
which, encouraged by the words
of Jesus your Son
on the Cross—*"Behold, your Mother"*—
wishes to entrust itself to your heavenly protection.

Now O Mother of the Church
and our mother
this community, in consecrating itself to you, offers you:
the innocence of the children,
the generosity and enthusiasm of the young people,
the suffering of the sick,
the solitude of the old people,
the labor of the workers,
the hardships of the unemployed,
the affections that are nurtured in the families.

O Mother, look down on
those who search for the meaning of existence,
the repentance of those who are lost
in sin,
the purposes and hopes
of those who seek the love
of the Father and live it,
the faithfulness and dedication of priests,

the prayers and the service of nuns,
and the zeal of those who are employed in the Apostolate
and in works of mercy.

You, Blessed Virgin,
who believed the Word of the Lord,
make us courageous witnesses of Christ:
may
our charity be authentic,
in order to lead unbelievers
into faith,
and reach them all.

O Mary, grant
that the civil community
may make progress in solidarity
and in justice,
and may its fraternity increase.
Help us reach the horizons
of hope,
all the way to the eternal realities of Heaven.

Most Holy Virgin,
we entrust ourselves to you, we beseech you
to grant that in every choice the Church
may bear witness to the Gospel,
in order to build up the Kingdom of Jesus Christ,
who lives and reigns for ever and ever.

April 27, 1991

Watch over the Church, which is continuously threatened by the spirit of the world

Holy Mother of the Redeemer,
Gate of Heaven, Star of the Sea,
help your people, who yearn to rise.
Yet again
we turn to you,
Mother of Christ,
and of the Church.
We gather at your feet
to thank you
for what you have done
in these difficult years
for the Church,
for each of us,
and for all humanity.

"Show thyself a Mother":
how many times have we called on you!
And today we are here to thank you,
because you have always listened to us.
You showed that you are our Mother:
Mother of the Church,
missionary along the paths of the earth
in expectation of the third Christian millennium.
Mother of men,
for the constant protection
that has averted disasters

and irreparable destruction,
and has encouraged progress
and improvements in modern society.
Mother of nations,
for the unhoped-for changes
that have given trust back to peoples
too long oppressed and humiliated.
Mother of life, for the many signs
with which you accompanied us,
defending us from evil
and from the power of death.
Mother of every man who struggles for the life
that does not die.
Mother of humanity
redeemed by the blood of Christ.
Mother of perfect love,
of hope and peace,
Holy Mother of the Redeemer.

"Show thyself a Mother":
Yes, continue to show that you are the Mother of us all,
because the world needs you.
The new situations
of peoples and the Church
are still precarious and unstable.
The danger exists
of replacing Marxism
with another form of atheism,
which, idolizing freedom,
tends to destroy

the roots of human and Christian morality.
Mother of hope, walk with us!
Walk with mankind
at the very end
of the twentieth century,
with men of every race and culture,
of every age and state.
Walk with peoples
toward solidarity and love,
walk with the young,
the protagonists of future days of peace.
The nations that have recently
regained their freedom
and are now engaged
in constructing their future
have need of you.
Europe needs you,
which from east to west
cannot find
its identity
without rediscovering
its common Christian roots.
The world needs you
to resolve
the many violent
conflicts that still
threaten it.

"Show thyself a Mother":
Show that you are the Mother of the poor,

of those who are dying of hunger and sickness,
of those who suffer injustice and tyranny,
of those who cannot find work, home, or refuge,
of those who are oppressed and exploited,
of those who despair or in vain seek
tranquillity far from God.
Help us to defend life,
the reflection of divine love,
help us to defend it forever,
from dawn to its natural sunset.
Show yourself the Mother of unity and peace.
May violence and injustice cease everywhere,
may harmony and unity
grow within families,
and respect and understanding among peoples;
may peace, true peace, reign upon the earth!
Mary, give Christ, our peace, to the world.
Do not let peoples reopen new abysses
of hatred and vengeance,
do not let the world yield to the seductions
of a false well-being
that perverts the value of the human person
and forever compromises
the natural resources of Creation.
Show yourself the Mother of hope!
Watch over the road that still awaits us.
Watch over men
and over the new situations of peoples
still threatened by the risk of war.
Watch over those responsible for nations

and those who rule the destiny of humanity.
Watch over the Church,
which is constantly threatened by the spirit of the world.

In collegial unity with the pastors, and
in communion with the entire people of God,
who are scattered to the far corners of the earth,
I today renew humanity's
filial trust in you.
To you we all with confidence entrust ourselves.
With you we hope to follow Christ,
the Redeemer of man: may our weariness
not weigh on us, nor our toil slacken us;
let not obstacles quench our courage,
nor sadness the joy in our hearts.
You, Mary, Mother of the Redeemer,
continue to show that you are the Mother of all,
watch over our path,
so that, full of joy, we may see
your Son in Heaven.
Amen.

ACT OF ENTRUSTMENT TO THE
VIRGIN OF FATIMA, MAY 13, 1991

To Mary, star of evangelization

O Mary, on the morning of Pentecost, when the Apostles,
by the action of the Holy Spirit,
initiated the work of evangelization,
you sustained them with prayer.
Preserve and protect us,
guiding the steps of the Church
today, too,
in this time of apprehension
and hope, when, obedient
to the mandate of the Lord, the Church
advances toward peoples and nations
in every corner of the earth
with the "happy news" of salvation.
Direct our choices in life,
comfort us in our hour of trial,
so that, faithful to God and humanity,
we may face with humility and daring the
mysterious pathways of the ether,
to bring to the mind
and heart of every person
the joyous news of Christ
the Redeemer of mankind.
O Mary, star of evangelization, walk with us!
Amen.

OCTOBER 21, 1992

Be a pilgrim with us, stay with us, and wait for us beyond the threshold of the new millennium

Immaculate Mother!
You are the dawn of new life in all Creation
and so from the very start Christians
have invoked you as the morning star.
Contemplating the sky
at the moment when night
gives way to day,
we see the first signs of the dawn that speaks of you.
Dawn has become your symbol
in the memory and imagination of believers.
You are the morning star,
the star of evangelization
"old" and "new."

Immaculate Mother of the new Creation!
You were the first to be redeemed by your Son,
redeemed to journey with us
on the pilgrimage of faith
to the Cross, on Golgotha.
You, the first and perfect witness
to the entire divine mystery of the Redemption
and renewal of man and the world,
on this day turn your gaze toward us,
for we have come to reveal to you our expectations

and ask for your intercession.
Look at Italy,
which seeks the paths of a just
and unified renewal.

Look at us!
Be a pilgrim with us
from the east to the west.
Stay with us, while the
second millennium
after the birth of the Word of the Most High
on the night in Bethlehem fades.
Stay with us, who are committed to
reducing the distance that, with the passing of the centuries, has divided
the fruit of the evangelization
that originated in Rome
and the Christian inheritance of Greece and Byzantium.
Look at us, who are concerned
with justice and peace.
Look at us Christians,
and help us to find unity throughout the globe,
especially on the old continent,
the crucible of ancient civilizations,
where Peter and Paul,
coming from Jerusalem through Antioch,
initiated
their apostolic commitment.
Look with us at
the Africa of St. Augustine, once a flowering oasis of the Gospel.

Help us in our dialogue
with the believers in the only God
who today inhabit those lands.

Look with us to the east,
to Oceania, Australia,
and New Zealand.
Look with us
at the vast continent of Asia,
where Christ is still little known,
and where we would like to meet
with our brothers and sisters
who are followers of the ancient legacies of Buddhism,
Hinduism, Taoism,
Shintoism, and Confucianism.
Do you think, perhaps, O Mother, that those peoples
do not know you, know nothing of you?
May they, too, see in you
the morning star.
Be for them, too, the herald
of the splendor of Christ, whom
they have not yet met,
but who remains on the horizon
of their search and their aspirations.

Allow us, O Mary,
to join your pilgrimage.
Immaculate Virgin!
Thanks to your presence
the Church remains new

and is constantly being renewed.
Mary, be a pilgrim with us
on the pathways of the world,
and even more through the generations.
Thanks to the young the Church is young
and is young again and again.

Next to God,
you are
the "Mother of all things made anew."
Upon you our gaze
of faith and hope is fixed.
You are, after Christ,
our greatest love.
You allow us to pass
through all experiences
toward the "new beginning."
And you wait for us beyond the threshold
of the new millennium,
so that Christ may be "yesterday, today, and forever!"

DECEMBER 8, 1993

Holy Virgin!
Queen of peace!
On this the first day of the year
the Liturgy honors you as the Mother of God,
a title that not only expresses
your greatness
but also constitutes our hope.
You carried in your womb the Son of God:
to you he cannot say no.
Obtain for us, O Mother, the gift of peace.
Inspire feelings and resolutions of peace
in all the families of the world.
With your powerful intercession, be
the Mother of our peace.
Amen.

JANUARY 1, 1994

Mary, watch over the young

Mary, Mother of the Church! Mary, Mother of the Church of young people, you were praying in the upper rooms with the Disciples of your Son when the Holy Spirit descended amid tongues of flame. Pray for us, so that *the flame of the love of God may be rekindled in our hearts* and in the hearts of the young everywhere.

Virgin full of grace! Immaculate from the first moment of your existence, now you share fully in the joy of Heaven. Watch over the young people gathered here and over all those who are one with us in the communion of the body of Christ. Pray that these young people may courageously accept the task that Christ your Son entrusts to them when he says: "As the Father has sent me, even so I send you."

Mary, Queen of Apostles! You watch over those whom your Son sends to be his messengers throughout the world. Inspire all young people to be *fervent witnesses* to the Gospel's message of salvation. With your help may they be able to share with others the new life that spreads from Christ's Cross, the hope that comforts every heart and the strength that grants the final victory over sin and death.

Mary of the New Advent! To you, Holy Mother of God, we raise our prayer.

JANUARY 15, 1995

O Mary,
bright dawn of the new world,
Mother of the living,
we entrust to you the *cause of life:*
O Mother, look down upon the number
of babies not allowed to be born,
of poor people whose lives are made difficult,
of men and women
who are victims of brutal violence,
of the elderly and the sick people killed by
indifference
or out of misguided mercy.
Grant that all who believe in your Son
may proclaim the *Gospel of life*
with honesty and love,
to the people of our time.
Obtain for them the grace to accept that Gospel
as a gift that is ever new,
the joy of celebrating it with gratitude
throughout their lives
and the courage to bear witness to it
resolutely, in order to build,
together with all people
of good will,
the civilization of truth and love,
to the praise and glory of God, the Creator
and lover of life.

EVANGELIUM VITAE
(ENCYCLICAL, MARCH 25, 1995)

Invocation to the Virgin Mary

Mary, image of the Church, the Bride without spot or wrinkle, which by imitating you "preserves with virginal purity, an integral faith, a firm hope, and a sincere charity," sustain consecrated persons on their journey toward the sole and eternal Blessedness.

To you, Virgin of the Visitation, we entrust them, so that they may go forth to meet human needs, to bring help, but above all to bring Jesus. Teach them to proclaim the marvels that the Lord accomplishes in the world, so that all peoples may extol the greatness of his name. Support them in their work for the poor, the hungry, those without hope, the little ones, and all who seek your Son with a sincere heart.

To you, our Mother, who wish for the spiritual and apostolic renewal of your sons and daughters in a response of love and complete dedication to Christ, we address our confident prayer. You who did the will of the Father, ever ready in obedience, courageous in poverty, receptive in fruitful virginity, obtain from your divine Son that all who have received the gift of following him in the consecrated life may be enabled to bear witness to that gift by their transfigured lives, as they joyously make their way, with all their brothers and sisters, to the heavenly homeland and the light that never grows dim.

We ask you this, that in everyone and in everything glory, adoration, and love may be given to the Most High Lord of all things, who is Father, Son, and Holy Spirit.

VITA CONSECRATA, 112

Hail, glorious Mother of the Redeemer

Hail, glorious Mother of the Redeemer, Ark of the Covenant, in whom the total mystery of the Redemption is fulfilled: in you the promise of Emmanuel, of God with us, became reality, and God became our brother.

Hail, humble Handmaiden of the Lord, who gave to men the Son of God, and, as an obedient woman, with your "let it be" taught us to do docilely all that he asks of us.

Hail, Holy Virgin, who accompanied and followed your divine Son, suffering and crucified, unto death, and at the foot of the Cross became "Our Mother," Mother of the Church and all humanity.

Hail, Virgin at prayer with the Apostles at the Last Supper: with your intercession you obtained for us the gift of the Holy Spirit, which renews Heaven and earth.

Hail, glorious Virgin, in the mystery of your Assumption into Heaven: in you God the Father first accomplished what he intends to do at the end of time for all who die in communion with his and your Son, Jesus Christ.

We salute you, Queen of the Angels and the Saints, who from Heaven intercede for us and sustain us on our earthly pilgrimage to the Promised Land: keep our faith alive, our hope steadfast, our love for God and our brothers and sisters ardent.

As we contemplate the mystery of your Assumption, O Mary, we learn to give earthly realities their proper value. Help us not to forget that our true and final dwelling place is Heaven, and support our efforts to make our shared life down here more fraternal and united. Make us workers for justice and makers of peace in the name of Christ, our true peace.

Holy Virgin, as you guide us like a luminous star toward the Great Jubilee of 2000, enable all men and women to recognize in Jesus, the blessed fruit of your womb, their Savior.

O clement, O pious, O sweet Virgin Mary!

AUGUST 15, 1996

To you, Virgin of Loreto, we trustfully turn our gaze.

We ask you, "our life, sweetness, and hope," for the grace to await the dawn of the third millennium with the same feelings that vibrated in your heart while you awaited the birth of your Son Jesus.

Your protection frees us from pessimism, letting us glimpse amid the shadows of our time the luminous traces of the Lord's presence.

To your maternal tenderness we entrust the tears, laments, and hopes of the sick. May the balm of comfort and hope bring relief to their wounds. May their pain, joined with that of Jesus, be transformed into an instrument of Redemption.

Your example leads us to make our lives a constant song of praise to God's love. Make us attentive to the needs of others, ready to bring aid to those who suffer, to be companions to those who are alone, builders of hope where the dramas of man are consummated.

At every stage of our journey, whether happy or sad, show us with a mother's affection "your Son Jesus, O clement, O pious, O sweet Virgin Mary."

Amen.

JUNE 29, 1997

Mary, young Daughter of Israel, who immediately answered yes to the Father's proposal, make these young people attentive and obedient to the will of God. You for whom virginity meant the total acceptance of divine love, enable them to discover the beauty and freedom of a virgin existence. You who possessed nothing in order to be rich only in God and his Word, free their hearts from every worldly attachment, so that the Kingdom of God may be their sole treasure, their sole passion.

Young Daughter of Zion, who, in love with God in your heart, remained forever a virgin, sustain in them and in all of us a forever youthful spirit of love. Virgin of sorrows, who remained at the Cross of your Son, generate in each of your children, as in the Apostle John, love stronger than death. Virgin Mother of he who is risen, make us all witnesses of the joy of Christ who lives forever.

OCTOBER 1, 1997

O Mary,
Mother of Mercy,
watch over all people,
so that the Cross of Christ
may not be emptied of its power,
so that man may not stray from the path of the good,
or become blind to sin,
but may put his hope ever more fully in God, who is
"rich in mercy."
May he carry out the good works
Prepared by God beforehand
and so live completely
"for praise of his glory."

VERITATIS SPLENDOR
(ENCYCLICAL, AUGUST 6, 1993)

O Virgin of Nazareth,
the "yes" spoken in youth
marked your existence
and it grew as did your life itself.
O Mother of Jesus,
in your free and joyous "yes"
and in your active faith
so many generations and so many teachers
have found inspiration and strength
for welcoming the Word of God
and for doing his will.
O Teacher of life,
teach young people
to pronounce the "yes"
that gives meaning to existence
and lets them discover the hidden "name" of God
in the heart of each of us.
O Queen of the Apostles,
give us wise teachers,
who will know how to love young people and help them grow,
guiding them to the encounter with Truth
that makes us free and happy.
Amen!

MESSAGE FOR THE WORLD DAY OF
PRAYER FOR VOCATIONS, 1995

Help us respect Creation

O Mary,
radiant with singular beauty,
help us appreciate and respect Creation.
You who are so beloved
by the people of the mountains,
and in these valleys
are worshiped in so many sanctuaries,
protect the valleys' inhabitants,
so that they may be faithful to their traditions
and at the same time open and hospitable.
Help us to make our lives
an ascension toward God
and to follow forever Jesus Christ, your Son,
who guides us to our goal,
where, in the new Creation,
we will enjoy the fullness of life and peace.

July 11, 1999

For Christian Unity

Praying for the unity of Christians
is a task that is within reach of
every Christian.
All Christians, without exception,
are engaged in striving for
the universal communion
which comes from our common baptism.

For the unity of all Christians

Let us pray for the unity of all Christians. This great gift that only God can grant can transform hearts, divisions, and the wounds of centuries, and expand the prayer that Jesus addressed to the Father for the unity of his Disciples: "That they may all be one; even as thou art in me, and I in thee." With this prayer we begin the ecumenical week, turning to our Christian brothers who are not yet fully united with us, and we invoke this unity as a gift from on high.

Amen!

JANUARY 19, 1992

Praying for unity is a task that is *within reach of every Christian.* Even if we cannot all share in every aspect of the search for unity (study, dialogues, practical contributions), we can all join in continual and harmonious prayer for the gift of unity. Parishes, religious communities, especially those of contemplative life, and individuals can do this. All Christians, without exception, are engaged in striving for the universal communion which comes from our common baptism.

JANUARY 24, 1990

A single community

Let us pray God, who in Jesus Christ wished to unite all men in a single community of salvation, to grant that his disciples may bear witness to unity in our time.

Let us therefore repeat:

Blessed are you, O Lord.

Lord, you sent your Only Begotten Son to redeem and save all humanity.

Blessed are you, O Lord.

You gave us your Spirit, you gather us in our communities.

Blessed are you, O Lord.

You wish all people to be your holy people; you dispense gifts and talents and call all to the unity of one body.

Blessed are you, O Lord.

Grant, O Lord, that we may turn to you with confidence as the Father, and say with one heart: Our Father.

JANUARY 18, 1989

Full unity

I invite you to pray with me for the full unity of all Christians.

That the life of Christians in the various churches and ecclesial communities may be nourished by your love,

we pray to you

Hear us, Lord.

That our common path toward the full unity of all Christians may be free from false fears,

we pray to you

Hear us, Lord.

That we may travel that path together in joy, shared trust, and mutual aid,

we pray to you

Hear us, Lord.

Obedient to the command of the Lord and formed to his divine teaching, we dare to say:

Our Father...

JANUARY 20, 1988

The one and only Church

Let us pray together for the restoration of the full unity of all Christians:

Let us pray to the Lord that Christians, despite their divisions, may increasingly strive to bear witness together to their faith in God the Father, Son, and Holy Spirit, so that the world may believe.

Let them be one, so that the world may believe.

Let us pray that Christians, in particular those who suffer in the name of Jesus, may give testimony to the living faith and advance toward the full profession of the common faith.

Let them be one, so that the world may believe.

Let us pray for Christians to unite so that justice and peace can be achieved in the world.

Let them be one, so that the world may believe.

Our Father, who are in Heaven, / look upon the aspirations of the hearts of your children; / hear our requests / and let all Christians / be united in your one and only Church. / For your Son Jesus Christ, / who with you, in the communion of the Holy Spirit, / lives and reigns for ever and ever.

Amen.

JANUARY 22, 1982

"May all find their home in you, Lord"

Let us say together:

May all find their home in you, Lord.

For all the baptized, so that with their lives they may proclaim your Kingdom to all peoples, let us pray.

For Christian families, so that they may bear witness to love and unity, let us pray.

For our Christian communities, that they may be for all a home of fraternity, let us pray.

For Christians scattered throughout the world, that they may be one, let us pray.

For all people, that they may find in your Church reconciliation and peace, let us pray.

Let us pray *(from the Byzantine Liturgy)*: / Lord, our God, / save your people, / and bless your inheritance; / keep in peace / your entire Church; / sanctify those who love your house. / In exchange, / glorify them with your power / and do not abandon us, who place our hope in you.

Amen.

JANUARY 20, 1982

Transcending divisions

—We ask the Lord to fortify in all Christians faith in Christ, the Savior of the world.

—We ask the Lord that with his gifts he sustain and guide Christians on the path of total unity.

—We ask the Lord for the gift of unity and peace for the world.

—Let us pray: / We beseech you, O Lord / for the gifts of your Spirit. Let us penetrate / the depths of the whole truth, / and let us share with others / the goods that you dispense.

Teach us to transcend our divisions. / Send us your Spirit / to lead all your children / to full unity / in full charity / and obedience to your will, / for Christ our Lord.

Amen.

JANUARY 21, 1981

That all may be one

Let us raise our prayer, and say together: *"That all may be one."*

So that, from now on, Christians may bear witness in common, to serve your Kingdom. Let us pray!

That all may be one.

That all Christian communities may come together in search of full unity. Let us pray!

That all may be one.

That the perfect unity of all Christians may be achieved, and that God may be glorified by all men in Christ the Lord. Let us pray!

That all may be one.

That all the peoples of the earth may overcome conflicts and selfishness and find complete reconciliation and peace in the Kingdom of God. Let us pray!

That all may be one.

Let us pray: / remember, O Lord, your Church: / deliver her from every evil; / make her perfect in your love; / sanctify her and shelter her from the four winds / in your Kingdom, / which you have prepared for her. Because yours is the power and the glory forever.

Amen.

JANUARY 23, 1980

The courage of unity

Dear brothers and sisters, let us unite in prayer with the following invocations, to which you are all invited to respond *Hear us Lord!*

—In the spirit of Christ, our Lord, let us pray for the Catholic Church, for the other churches, for all humanity.

Hear us, Lord!

—Let us pray for all those who suffer persecution in the cause of justice and for those who strive for liberty and peace.

Hear us, Lord!

—Let us pray for those who practice a ministry in the Church, for those who have special responsibilities in society, and for all who serve the weak and defenseless.

Hear us, Lord!

—We ask God to give us the courage to persevere in our commitment to achieve the unity of all Christians.

Hear us, Lord!

Lord God / we have trust in you. / Grant that we may act in ways that are pleasing to you. / Grant that we may be faithful servants of your glory. /

Amen.

JANUARY 17, 1979

The path of Christians toward full communion requires the commitment of each one; above all, it requires prayer. Beyond what is humanly possible, *unity is a gift of God.* The Second Vatican Council has already underlined this, affirming that the "holy purpose of reconciling all Christians in the unity of the one and only Church of Christ is beyond human talents and strengths." We must therefore place our hopes in Christ's prayer for the Church, in the Father's love for us, and in the strength of the Holy Spirit.

Prayer offers the concrete possibility of sharing in an undertaking that permeates the consciousness of every believer, independent of his service and of the role that he occupies in the Church.

Also today we would like to ask the Lord to grant his disciples the gift of full unity. We do so by repeating some beautiful phrases from the prayer that was said at Santiago de Compostela:

> O Holy Trinity of love:
> we gather to give thanks to you
> for the gift of *koinonia**
> which we welcome as the first fruits
> of your Kingdom . . .
> We come to you in the expectation
> that we may enter
> more profoundly
> into the joy of *koinonia.*

. . .

* *Koinonia:* Communion of the Holy Spirit; Christian fellowship.

We come to you in trust,
to pledge ourselves again
to your design of love,
justice, and *koinonia*...

Here is our prayer and our pledge. May the Lord give all Christians renewed urgency in pursuit of that full, visible communion for which Christ gave his life.

JANUARY 19, 1994

For Vocations

The Church is missionary
by her very nature,
for Christ's mandate
is not something contingent or external
but reaches the very heart of the Church.

Redemptoris Missio, 62
(Encyclical, September 7, 1990)

Pray, call, respond

Lord Jesus,
who called those you wanted,
call many of us
to work with you.

You,
who enlightened with your Word
those whom you called,
enlighten us with the gift of faith in you.

You,
who have sustained us in difficulties,
help us to overcome
our difficulties as young people in these times.

And if you call one of us
to dedicate himself completely to you,
may your love warm this vocation
from its birth
and make it grow and persevere
to the end.
So let it be.

1979

Evangelize, reflect, pray

Let us pray

together with the Most Holy Virgin, trusting in her intercession.

Let us pray

that the holy mysteries of the Rising and of the Holy Spirit may enlighten many generous people, ready and willing to serve the Church.

Let us pray

for the pastors and for their helpers, so that they may find the right words in which to bring the faithful the message of the priestly and consecrated life.

Let us pray

that in all areas of the Church the faithful may believe with renewed fervor in the evangelical ideal of the priest who is completely devoted to building up the Kingdom of God, and that they may encourage such vocations with decisive generosity.

Let us pray

for young people, to whom the Lord addresses the call to follow him more nearly, so that they may not be led astray by the things of this world but will open their hearts to the friendly voice that calls them; so that they may be able to devote themselves for their whole life, "with an undivided heart," to Christ, to the Church, to other souls; so that they may believe that grace bestows on them strength for such giving, and that they may see the beauty and grandeur of the priestly, religious, and missionary life.

Let us pray

for families, that they may succeed in creating a Christian climate that fosters the important religious choices of their children. At the same time, we thank the Lord from the bottom of our hearts, because in recent years, in many parts of the world, young people, and others, are responding in increasing numbers to the divine call.

Let us pray

that all priests and religious may be to those who are called an example and an inspiration by their availability and their humble eagerness "to accept the gifts of the Holy Spirit and to bestow on others the fruits of love and peace, to give them that certainty of faith from which derives a profound comprehension of the sense of human life and the capacity to introduce a moral order into the lives of individuals and their environments."

1980

The Church prays for *priestly and religious vocations.* This is a problem that we cannot resolve except by appealing to grace, whose fullness is in Christ crucified and risen.

Let us all pray that the ecclesiastical seminaries and novitiates may be filled, so that the individual churches, and the communities—parishes, religious congregations—may look confidently toward the future, in the certainty of having those workers whom the Lord sends out "into his harvest"; priests, who, dedicating themselves exclusively to the Kingdom of God, will celebrate the Eucharist, preach the Word of the Lord, and carry out the pastoral ministry; and men and women who dedicate their lives completely to the divine Spouse, in the spirit of poverty, chastity and obedience, as witnesses to "the future world," which they are impelled toward by an infinite love for their neighbor.

Let us all pray that young people, boys and girls, may discover in themselves *the grace of a vocation,* as a special gift of the Church, a gift that Christ himself instills in their hearts; and that they may follow that call without turning back and without fear of their own weakness, or of the spirit of this world, or of the "prince of darkness."

If we pray for this, then we may be certain: the Lord of the harvest will respond to our petition if we show total obedience to Christ.

Not otherwise. Not otherwise. *So we cannot secretly harbor suspicions or doubts* about the essence of the ministerial priesthood, about the justice of the centuries-old practice of our Church, which links the priesthood to willingness to serve Christ and the Church "with an undivided heart." We cannot doubt the power of Christ, the action of his grace. We must think all the way to the end with him, accepting that what seems impossible to men is nevertheless possible to God.

Thus we must pray for vocations, and we must pray without reserve, trusting in this grace, whose fulfillment is in Christ, the chosen Son of the Father. *Praying this way means to be converted.*

MARCH 2, 1980

And now, dear brothers and sisters, let us join with *the whole Church,* which on this Sunday prays in a special way *for vocations.* The dioceses pray. The religious congregations pray. All those who love Christ and his Church pray. The Church, everywhere and always, needs priests, chosen from among men and established for the good of humanity.

It also needs *nuns* and *monks,* who live according to the evangelical counsels in total dedication to Christ. He is the same Lord Jesus who taught us that we must pray to the Lord of the harvest "that he send laborers into the harvest." This *harvest is plentiful.* It is immense. The petition, too, must be immense, and the prayer of the entire Church for laborers, who are indispensable for the harvest.

Let us pray for vocations, reciting the Easter greeting: "Queen of Heaven, rejoice." What is the most convincing testimony to the *Paschal maturity* of the Church—in every dimension: parish, diocese, congregation, nation, continent—what is, I repeat, the best testimony to this paschal joy, if not the increase in vocations? May the risen Christ / prevail in many young hearts; may *his call, "Follow me!," bring victory!* May the humility and faith of the whole Church, entrusted to the Mother of God, bear the desired fruit.

APRIL 27, 1980

Particular churches and vocations

Brothers and sisters,
with our common prayer,
wide as the world,
strong as our faith,
enduring as the charity
that the Holy Spirit
has poured into our hearts:

We praise the Lord,
who has enriched his Church with the gift of the priesthood, with the many forms of consecrated life, and with innumerable other graces for the edification of his people and service to humanity.

We give thanks to the Lord,
who continues to dispense his calls, to which many young people, and others, in these years and in various areas of the Church, are responding with increasing generosity.

We ask forgiveness of the Lord
for our weaknesses and infidelities, which perhaps discourage others from responding to his call.

We beg the Lord fervently
that he may grant to the pastors of souls, to men and women religious, to missionaries and other consecrated people the gifts of hope, counsel, and prudence in calling others to serve

God and the Church; and may he grant, equally, to a growing number of young people, and others, the generosity and courage to persevere.

We raise this our humble
and confident prayer,
entrusting it to the intercession
of Most Holy Mary,
Mother of the Church
Queen of the clergy,
the shining model for every soul
consecrated to the service of the people of God.

1981

To you, Mary, we say again: "I am entirely yours"

O Mother, Mother of God, Mother of the Church, / in this hour so significant for us / we are one heart and one soul: like Peter, the Apostles, our brothers and sisters, / may we join in prayer, with you, at the Last Supper.

We entrust to you our life, / to you, who welcomed with total faithfulness the Word of God / and devoted yourself to his plan of salvation and grace, / adhering with complete docility to the action of the Holy Spirit; / to you, who received from your Son the mission / to accept and watch over the Disciple he loved / to you we repeat, each of us, I am entirely yours, / so that you may take on our consecration / and join it to that of Jesus and to yours, / as an offering to God the Father, for the life of the world.

We implore you, watch over the needs of your children, / as you did at Cana, when you took to heart / the situation of that family. / What your family needs most today / is vocations: presbyterial, deaconal, religious, and missionary. / With your "supplicant's power," touch / the hearts of many of our brothers, / so that they may hear, understand, respond to the voice of the Lord. / Repeat to them, in the depths of their conscience, the command given to the servants at Cana: / Do whatever he tells you.

We will be ministers of God and of the Church, / who have vowed to evangelize, sanctify, feed our brothers and sisters: / teach us, give us the attitudes of the Good Shepherd; / nourish our apostolic devotion and make it grow; / fortify and constantly regenerate our love for those who suffer; / enlighten and vivify our offering of virginity for the Kingdom of Heaven; / instill and preserve in us the sense of fraternity and communion.

Along with our own lives we entrust to you, our Mother, / those of our parents and families; / those of our brothers and sisters whom we will reach with our ministry, / so that your maternal concern / may precede our steps toward them / and keep our path directed toward the homeland, / which Christ, your Son and our Lord, prepared for us with his Redemption. Amen.

APRIL 18, 1982

Life begets life

Lord Jesus, Good Shepherd,

who offered your life, so that all might have life, give us, the community of believers scattered throughout the world, the abundance of your life and make us capable of bearing witness to it and of communicating it to others.

Lord Jesus,

give the abundance of your life to all persons consecrated to you in service to the Church: make them happy in their giving, tireless in their ministry, generous in their sacrifice; and may their example open other hearts to hear your call and follow it.

Lord Jesus,

give the abundance of your life to Christian families, so that they may be fervent in faith and ecclesial service, thus encouraging the birth and development of new consecrated vocations.

Lord Jesus,

give the abundance of your life to all people, especially young men and women whom you call to serve you; enlighten them in their choices; help them in difficulties; sustain them in faith; render them eager and courageous in offering their lives, according to your example, so that others may have life.

May the Most Holy Virgin,

Mother of God and of the Church, support this petition with your powerful intercession and make it pleasing to you.

1982

The Church prays for priestly vocations

On this Sunday the Church prays *in particular for priestly vocations.* Following the signs of her Teacher she prays the Lord of the harvest to send laborers into the harvest.

Returning to the upper rooms on the day of the Resurrection, the Church prays that the Good Shepherd will send and continue to send new bands of his Disciples on this mission, which he himself received from the Father.

The Church prays:

—that this call may reach many young hearts: "Receive the Holy Spirit. If you forgive the sins of any, they are forgiven; if you retain the sins of any, they are retained."

—that through the *power of the Holy Spirit* servants of Christ and those who administer the mysteries of God will be born among the people and nations of the world.

I return to the words of the prayer for Holy Thursday in the year of our Lord 1982:

This sponsal love of the Redeemer, this salvific love of the Bridegroom, makes fruitful all the "hierarchical and charismatic gifts" with which the Holy Spirit "provides for and directs" the Church.

Is it possible, Lord, that we can doubt this love of yours?

Can anyone who lets himself be guided by living faith in the founder of the Church possibly doubt this love, to which the Church owes all its spiritual vitality?

Can we possibly doubt

—that you can, and desire to, give your Church true "ministers of the mysteries of God" and, above all, true ministers of the Eucharist?

—that you can, and desire to, awaken in the souls of men and women, especially the young, the charism of priestly service, as it has been accepted and carried out in the tradition of the Church?

—that you can, and desire to, awaken in these souls, along with aspirations to the priesthood, a willingness to accept the gift of celibacy for the Kingdom of Heaven, which entire generations of priests of the Catholic Church displayed in the past and still do today?

Queen of Heaven, rejoice! O Mother of the one who is risen, let us enjoy the ever renewed gifts of the Paschal Mystery! Ask that they may be given to us by eternal and merciful Love!

When Christ says: "Receive the Holy Spirit," may those who are called know how to accept this ineffable gift.

MAY 2, 1982

The Holy Spirit and vocations

Lord Jesus,

hear our invocation:

—through your Spirit, renew your Church so that it may with increasing abundance offer to the world the fruits of your Redemption;

—through your Spirit, fortify in their holy offerings those who have dedicated their lives to the Church: in the presbyterate, in the deaconate, in the religious life, in the missionary institutes, in the other forms of consecrated life, and, having called them to your service, make them perfect cooperators in your work of salvation;

—through your Spirit, multiply the calls to your service: you read in our hearts and know that many are disposed to follow you and work for you; give the young, and others, the generosity necessary to welcome your call, the strength to accept the renunciations that it requires, the joy of carrying the Cross that is joined to their choice, as you first carried it, in the certainty of Resurrection.

We pray to you, Lord Jesus,

together with your Most Holy Mother Mary who was near you in the hour of your redeeming sacrifice;

we pray to you for her intercession so that many of us, today as well, may have the courage and humility, the faithfulness and the love to answer "yes" as she did when she was called to collaborate with you in your mission of universal salvation.

So let it be.

1983

Prayer and action

O Jesus, good Shepherd,

accept our praise and our humble thanks for all the vocations that, through your Spirit, you continuously bestow on your Church.

Help the bishops, the presbyters, the missionaries, and all consecrated people: may they be an example of the life truly devoted to the Gospel.

Make those who are preparing for the sacred ministry and the consecrated life strong and steadfast in their purpose.

Multiply the workers of the Gospel so that your name may be proclaimed to all peoples.

Protect the young people of our families and our communities: may they be ready and generous in following you.

Turn your gaze upon them today, too, and call them.

Grant to all who have been called the strength to abandon everything and choose you alone who are love. Forgive the conflicts and infidelities of those whom you have chosen.

Hear, O Christ,

our invocations for the intercession of Most Holy Mary, your Mother and Queen of the Apostles. May she who, having believed and responded generously, has been the cause of our joy, attend with her presence and her example those whom you call to serve your Kingdom.

Amen.

1984

Young people, Christ calls you

God our Father,
we entrust to you the young men
and young women of the world,
with their problems,
aspirations, and hopes.
Keep your loving gaze on them
and make them workers of peace
and builders of the civilization of love.
Call them to follow Jesus, your Son.
Help them to understand the value
of giving their lives fully
for you and for humanity.
Let their response be
generous and eager.
Accept also, Lord,
our praise and our prayer
for the young people who,
following the example of Mary, the Mother of the Church,
believed in your word
and are preparing for Holy Orders,
for the profession of the evangelical counsels,
for the missionary commitment.
Help them to understand that the call
you have given them
is always present and urgent.
Amen.

1985

Young people,

if *that call* reaches your heart, don't silence it! *Let it mature to become a vocation!* Collaborate with it through prayer and fidelity to the commandments! *"The harvest, in fact, is plentiful."* There is an enormous need for many to be reached by the call of Christ: "Follow me." There is an enormous *need for priests* after God's own heart—and the Church and the world of today have an enormous need *for testimony of the life given to God without reserve:* testimony of that sponsal love of Christ himself, which in a special way makes the Kingdom of God present among men and brings it closer to the world.

Allow me, therefore, to complete the words of Christ the Lord *on the harvest which is plentiful.* Yes, this harvest of the Gospel is plentiful, this harvest of salvation! . . . *"But the workers are few!"* Perhaps today that is felt more than in the past, especially in some nations, and in some institutes of consecrated life, and so forth.

"Pray therefore the Lord of the harvest to send out laborers into his harvest," Christ continues. These words, especially in our time, become a program of prayer and action to encourage priestly and religious vocations. With this plan *the Church turns to you, to young people.* You, too: ask! And if the fruit of this prayer of the Church is born in the depths of your heart, listen to the Teacher who says: "Follow me!"

MARCH 31, 1985

Let us not forget this purpose of our prayers: let us pray and help others pray for priestly and religious vocations.

The whole Church really needs such prayers. *"Pray the Lord of the harvest to send out laborers into his harvest."*

That is why we are gathered here, like the Apostles after the Ascension.

Let us pray *with Mary,* for she is the first called to the threshold of the New Testament. She is the model of the heart that pleases God, the family of God. She remains, for priests, the model of cooperation with the work of Christ, of openness to the Holy Spirit. She is the model of a life consecrated to the Lord. She directs the disciples to Christ so that they may adhere to him with love and do all that he tells them. It is easy for us to say with her, in the "Our Father," *"Thy will be done."*

With her, in the Rosary, we follow step by step the joyful, sorrowful, and glorious life of her Son, through her own life.

With Mary, we open our hearts to the Holy Spirit.

Let us pray in the name of Christ. Perhaps, up to now, you have not asked enough when you invoked the name of Christ. You must be confident that "nothing is impossible for God."

"Ask and you will receive, that your joy may be full."

Yes, vocations are the fruit of prayer, they are the source of joy in the Church.

Amen.

MAY 18, 1985

May you be a living community

O Jesus, Good Shepherd,

in all the parish communities inspire priests and deacons, men and women religious, consecrated lay people and missionaries, according to the needs of the whole world, which you love and wish to save.

We entrust to you especially our communities: create in us the spiritual climate of the first Christians, so that we may be a circle of prayer in loving welcome of the Holy Spirit and his gifts.

Help our pastors and all consecrated persons. Guide the steps of those who have generously welcomed your call and are preparing for Holy Orders or the profession of the evangelical counsels.

Turn your loving gaze upon many sympathetic young people and call them to your following. Help them to understand that only in you can they completely fulfill themselves.

In entrusting these great interests of your heart to the powerful intercession of Mary, our mother and the model for all vocations, we entreat you to sustain our faith, in the certainty that the Father will grant that which you yourself have commanded us to ask for.

Amen.

1986

Signs of God's love

Our Lord God, let the visible and courageous presence of the religious in the world be an eloquent sign of your love. Among the disciples you have chosen and established in the religious life, may the clarity of their message, the gift without return of themselves, the disinterest of their service, their faithfulness in prayer be seen by young people as calls to your grace.

May the institutes that have given so much to your Church see the flowering of many vocations, so that their indispensable mission may continue.

Lord Jesus Christ, let those whom you have wished to call your friends know fully the joy that you have promised: the joy of praising you, the joy of serving their brothers and sisters, the joy of abiding in your love.

To all your religious children, clerics and lay brothers, your daughter religious, to the members of secular institutes, grant, Lord, the support of your grace and the abundance of your blessings.

OCTOBER 6, 1986

Consider the call

Lord Jesus,

Just as you called the first Disciples to make them fishers of men, so may you continue to make your sweet call heard today: "Come, follow me!"

Give young men and women the grace to respond readily to your voice.

Sustain our bishops, priests, and consecrated people in their Apostolic labors. Let our seminarians persevere, along with all who are achieving the ideal of a life totally devoted to your service.

Reawaken in our communities the missionary commitment. Lord, send laborers into your harvest and do not let mankind go astray because there are not enough pastors, missionaries, and others vowed to the cause of the Gospel.

Mary, Mother of the Church,

model for every vocation, help us to answer "yes" to the Lord who calls us to collaborate in the divine plan of salvation.

1987

Mary, the mediator of vocations

We turn to you, Mother of the Church.

To you, who with your "let it be" opened the door to the presence of Christ in the world, in history, and in our souls, welcoming in humble silence and total compliance the call of the Almighty.

Today again, enable men and women to hear the inviting voice of your Son: "Follow me!"

Help them find the courage to leave their families, their occupations, their earthly hopes, and follow Christ on the path he has traced.

Hold out your maternal hand to the missionaries scattered throughout the world, to the men and women religious who help the old, the sick, the crippled, the orphans; to those who are committed to teaching, to the members of secular institutes, silent fermenters of good works; to those who in closed orders live in faith and love and ask for the salvation of the world.

Amen.

1988

Call them, take them, send them out

Lord Jesus Christ,

shepherd of our souls, who continue to call with your loving gaze so many young men and women who live amid the difficulties of the modern world, open their minds so that, among the many voices clamoring around them, they may recognize your voice, which, both gentle and powerful, is unmistakable and which says again, today: "Come, follow me!"

Encourage young people in their enthusiasm to be generous and make them aware of the expectations of their brothers and sisters who call for solidarity and peace, truth and love.

Direct the hearts of young people toward evangelical radicalism, which can reveal to modern man the immense riches of your charity.

Call them with your goodness, to draw them to you! Hold them with your sweetness, to welcome them to you! Send them out with your truth, to keep them with you!

Amen.

1989

The gift of the spirit

O Spirit of Truth,
who came to us at Pentecost
to form us in the school of the divine Word,
accomplish in us the mission
for which the Son sent you.
Fill every heart
and inspire in the young a yearning
toward that which is authentically great
and good in life,
the desire for evangelical perfection,
the passion for the salvation of souls.
Sustain the workers in the harvest
and give spiritual rewards to their efforts
on the path of the good.
Make our hearts
completely free and pure,
and help us to live fully
the following of Christ,
to taste as your ultimate gift
the joy that has no end.
Amen.

1990

The vocation of the catechists

O Jesus,
Good Shepherd of the Church,
to you we entrust our catechists;
may they, under the guidance of the bishops and priests,
be able to lead those who are entrusted to them
to discover the authentic significance
of the Christian life as a vocation,
so that, open and attentive to your voice,
they may follow you generously.
Bless our parishes,
transform them into living communities,
so that through prayer and the liturgical life,
attentive and faithful listening to your Word,
and generous and fruitful charity,
they may become a favorable ground
for the birth and development
of an abundant harvest of vocations.
O Mary,
Queen of the Apostles,
bless the young,
let them share in your docile listening
to the voice of God
and help them to utter, like you,
a generous and unconditional "yes"
to the mystery of love and election
that the Lord calls them to.

1991

Prayer for seminarians

Lord,
enable these future priests
to have a personality that is honest, and
rich in virtue,
in the semblance of Jesus Christ.
Enable them to be men of God,
and, like Jesus, men for others.
Instill in their hearts
a real love for the divine Word,
for the Eucharist and for prayer,
for the Church and for the doctrine of salvation
that she preserves and faithfully proclaims.
Enable them, finally,
in preparation
for their future ministry,
to be more holy every day.
Amen.

OCTOBER 15, 1991

Draw them to your heart!

O Virgin Mary,
to you we commend our young people,
especially those who have been called
to follow your Son more nearly.
You know how many difficulties
they must face,
how many struggles, how many obstacles.
Help them, as well, to respond with
their "yes" to the divine call,
as you answered the angel's appeal.
Draw them to your heart,
so that with you they may understand
the beauty and joy that await them,
when the Almighty calls them
to his intimacy.
He constitutes them as witnesses to your Love
and enables them to gladden the Church
by their consecration.
O Virgin Mary,
grant all of us the power to rejoice with you,
when we see that the love brought by your Son
is welcomed, protected, and loved in return.
Grant that we may also
see in our time
the wonders of the mysterious action
of the Holy Spirit.
Amen.

1992

Mother of priests

O Mary,
Mother of Jesus Christ and Mother of priests,
accept this title which we bestow on you
to celebrate your motherhood
and to contemplate with you the priesthood
of your Son and of your sons,
O Holy Mother of God.

O Mother of Christ,
to the Messiah-priest you gave a body of flesh
through the anointing of the Holy Spirit
for the salvation of the poor and the contrite of heart;
guard priests in your heart and in the Church,
O Mother of the Savior.

O Mother of Faith,
you accompanied to the Temple the Son of Man,
the fulfillment of the promises given to the fathers;
give to the Father for his glory
the priests of your Son,
O Ark of the Covenant.

O Mother of the Church,
in the midst of the Disciples in the upper room
you prayed to the Spirit
for the new people and their shepherds;
obtain for the Order of Presbyters

a full measure of gifts,
O Queen of the Apostles.

O Mother of Jesus Christ,
you were with him at the beginning
of his life and mission,
you sought the Master among the crowd,
you stood beside him when he was lifted
up from the earth
consumed as the one Eternal Sacrifice,
and you had John, your son, near at hand;
accept from the beginning those
who have been called,
protect their growth,
in their life ministry accompany
your sons,
O Mother of priests.
Amen.

Pastores Dabo Vobis
(Apostolic Exhortation, March 25, 1992)

The Virgin of Evangelization

Let us pray to the Virgin of Evangelization, that she may inspire fearless and generous *evangelizers* in our time; let us pray that there is no shortage of priests after Christ's own heart.

The promotion of priestly and religious vocations has to be a pastoral priority for the bishops, supported by prayer and by the ecclesial commitment of the faithful. The condition, in fact the principal condition, of the *New Evangelization* is that there be many qualified evangelizers. Furthermore, a decisive impetus must be given to the pastoral vocational work, and the subject of the *seminaries,* both diocesan and religious, must be confronted with wisdom and hope, as must the problem of the *permanent formation* of the clergy. All of that must be done according to the directions given in the recent post-synodal Apostolic Exhortation *Pastores Dabo Vobis.*

We entrust these intentions of ours to the Virgin, "the Sanctuary of the Most Holy Trinity." We ask for holiness in our *priests* and pastoral fervor. May the *Virgin of Evangelization* accompany them and guide them on their path as evangelizers. May the Madonna help all of us to be in every circumstance witnesses of the Gospel of salvation.

JUNE 14, 1992

Pastores dabo vobis

Pastores dabo vobis: with these words the whole Church addresses you, who are the Lord of the harvest, asking for laborers for your harvest, which is plentiful. Good Shepherd, long ago you sent the first workers into your harvest. They were twelve. Now that almost two millenniums have passed, and their voice has traveled to the ends of the earth, we, too, feel profoundly the need to pray that there will be no shortage of successors to them for our time—and, in particular, no shortage of men in the ministerial priesthood, who build up the Church with the power of the Word of God and the Sacraments; who in your name administer the Eucharist, from which the Church continually grows, the Church which is your Body.

We thank you, because the temporary crisis of vocations, in the context of the universal Church, is on the way to being resolved. With great joy we have seen a strong renewal of vocations in various parts of the globe: in the young churches, but also in the many nations of a centuries-old Christian tradition, not to mention places where, in our century, the Church has been harshly persecuted. But we raise our prayer with special fervor as we think of those societies in which the climate of secularization dominates, in which the spirit of this world inhibits the action of the Holy Spirit, so that the seed scattered in the souls of the young either does not take root or does not mature. For those societies, in particular, we implore you even more eagerly: *"Send forth your Spirit and renew the face of the earth."*

The Church thanks you, O divine Bridegroom, because from the earliest times she accepted the call to consecrated celibacy for the sake of the Kingdom of God; because for centuries she has preserved the charism of the celibacy of priests. We thank you for the Second Vatican Council and for the recent Synods of bishops, which, affirming this charism, pointed to it as a just path for the Church of the future. We are aware how fragile are the vessels in which we carry this treasure—yet we believe in the power of the Holy Spirit who works through the grace of the Sacrament in each of us. Even more fervently we ask that we may be able to collaborate with this power and persevere.

We ask you, who are the Spirit of Christ the Good Shepherd, to remain faithful to this particular inheritance of the Latin Church. *"Do not quench the Spirit,"* the Apostle tells us. We therefore ask not to fall into doubt or sow doubts in others, not to become—God preserve us!—supporters of different choices and of a different spirituality for life and the mystery of the priesthood. St. Paul says again: *"And do not grieve the Holy Spirit of God..."*

Pastores dabo vobis!

We pray to you to forgive all our sins before the Holy Mystery of your priesthood in our life. We ask that we may be able to collaborate and persevere in this "plentiful harvest," and do all that is necessary to inspire and nurture vocations. Above all, we ask you to help us pray with constancy. You yourself said: *"Pray therefore the Lord of the harvest to send out laborers into his harvest."*

As we confront this world, which in various ways displays indifference toward the Kingdom of Heaven, may we be accompanied by the certainty that you, Good Shepherd, instilled in the hearts of the Apostles: *"Be of good cheer; I have overcome the world!"* This is—in spite of everything—the same world that your Father loved so much that he gave to it you, his Only Begotten Son.

Mother of the Divine Son, Mother of the Church, Mother of all peoples—pray with us! Pray for us!

NOVEMBER 30, 1992

To the Shepherd of our souls

Lord Jesus Christ,

Good Shepherd of our souls, you who know your sheep and know how to touch our hearts, open the minds and hearts of those young people who seek and expect words of truth for their lives;

make them feel that only in the mystery of your Incarnation will they find full enlightenment;

inspire courage in those who know where to seek the truth but fear that your demands are too exacting;

rouse the spirits of those young people who would like to follow you but are unable to overcome doubts and fears, and end up following other voices and dead-end paths.

You who are the Word of the Father, the Word that creates and saves, the Word that enlightens and sustains our hearts, with your Spirit overcome the resistance and hesitations of indecisive souls;

let them know that you are calling for the courage of the loving response: "Here I am, send me!"

Virgin Mary,

young Daughter of Israel, with your motherly love support those young people whom the Father has caused to hear his Word; sustain those who are already consecrated. Let them say with you the "yes" of a joyous and irrevocable self-giving.

Amen.

1993

Lord Jesus Christ,
sent by the Father and anointed by the Spirit,
who entrusted to your Disciples
the proclamation of salvation,
so that it would reach the ends of the earth
and to the end of time,
inspire a new spring of vocations.

You who know each one by name
and have the words of eternal life,
renew the call to leave everything and follow you,
so that many young people will consecrate themselves to you
in the priesthood
and in the consecrated life,
dedicating themselves completely
in the service of the Gospel.

You who entrust to your friends
the words of the Father,
be the one Lord and Teacher
of all who are called.
Bestow on the ecclesial communities
the gifts of your Spirit,
so that a new
generation of Apostles
may proclaim your Resurrection
to all people
and unite them in your Church.

. . .

Renew in all the baptized
the pressing call
to the New Evangelization,
so that they may be witnesses of your Truth
and of your Life,
among men and women
in our time.
We ask you for the intercession
of the Virgin Mary,
the model of total dedication to your service
and the Mother of all those called
to be Apostles of your Kingdom.
Amen.

MESSAGE TO THE 1ST LATIN-AMERICAN
CONGRESS FOR THE VOCATIONS,
FEBRUARY 2, 1994

Lord, you wished to save mankind
and you founded the Church
as a communion of brothers and sisters
united in your Love.
Continue to walk in our midst
and call those whom you have chosen
to be the voice of your Holy Spirit,
and the leaven of a more just and fraternal society.
Obtain for us from the Heavenly Father the spiritual guides
our communities need:
true priests of the living God who,
illuminated by your Word, will be able to speak of you
and teach others to speak with you.
Make your Church grow
By means of a flourishing of consecrated men and women
who will give all things over to you,
so that you may save all.
May our communities celebrate
the Eucharist
in song and praise, as thanksgiving
to your glory and goodness,
and may they know how to walk the paths of the world
to communicate joy and peace,
the precious gifts of your salvation.
O Lord, turn your gaze
upon the whole human family
and show your mercy
to the men and women
who in prayer
and righteous living

seek you even though they have not yet encountered you:
show yourself to them as the way
that leads to the Father,
the truth that makes us free,
the life that has no end.
Lord, grant that we may live in your Church
in the spirit of faithful service
and total offering,
so that our testimony
will be credible and bear fruit.
Amen!

MESSAGE FOR THE WORLD DAY OF
PRAYER FOR VOCATIONS, 1996

Holy and provident Father,

you are the Lord of the vineyard and of the harvest
and give to each one
a just reward for his work.
In your design of love
you call men to work with you
for the salvation of the world.
We thank you for Jesus Christ,
your living Word,
who has redeemed us from our sins
and is come among us to help us
in our poverty.
Guide the flock to which you have promised
possession of the Kingdom.
Send new workers into your harvest
and instill in the hearts of pastors
faithfulness to your plan of salvation,
perseverance in their vocation,
and holiness in their lives.
Christ Jesus,
who on the shores of the Sea of Galilee
called the Apostles
and made them the foundation of the Church
and bearers of your Gospel,
in our day, sustain your people
on their journey.
Give courage to those
whom you call to follow you

in the priesthood
and the consecrated life,
so that they may enrich God's field
with the wisdom of your Word.
Make them docile instruments of your love
in daily service to their brothers and sisters.
Spirit of Holiness,
who pour your gifts on all believers
and, especially,
on those called to be Christ's ministers,
help young people discover the beauty
of the divine call.
Teach them the true way of prayer,
which is nourished by the Word of God.
Help them to read the signs of the times,
in order to be faithful interpreters of the Gospel
and bearers of salvation.
Mary, Virgin who listened,
and Virgin of the Word made flesh in your womb,
help us to be open
to the Word of the Lord,
so that, having been welcomed and meditated on,
it may grow in our hearts.
Help us to live, like you,
the beatitudes of believers
and to dedicate ourselves with unceasing charity
to evangelizing those
who seek your Son.
Grant that we may serve every person,
becoming servants of the Word we have heard,

so that, by remaining faithful to it,
we may find our happiness in living it.
Amen!

MESSAGE FOR THE WORLD DAY OF
PRAYER FOR VOCATIONS, 1997

Good Father,
in Christ your Son you reveal to us your love,
you embrace us as your children,
and you offer us the possibility of discovering
in your will the features
of our true face.
Holy Father,
you call us to be holy
as you are holy.
We pray that you may never allow your Church
to lack holy priests and Apostles
who, with the Word and the Sacraments,
will open the way to the encounter with you.
Merciful Father, give
to lost humanity men and women who,
through the witness of a life transfigured
to the image of your Son,
may walk joyously with
their other brothers and sisters
toward our heavenly homeland.
Our Father,
with the voice of your Holy Spirit,
and trusting in the maternal
intercession of Mary,
we earnestly beseech you:
send to your Church priests,
who will be courageous witnesses
of your infinite bounty.
Amen!

MESSAGE FOR THE WORLD DAY OF
PRAYER FOR VOCATIONS, 1999

Prayer of gratitude for the gift of the priesthood

"Te deum laudamus,
Te Dominum confitemur..."
We praise you and we thank you, O God:
all the earth adores you.
We, your ministers,
with the voices of the Prophets
and the chorus of the Apostles,
proclaim you Father and Lord of life,
of every form of life
which comes from you alone.
We recognize you, O Most Holy Trinity,
as the birthplace and beginning of our vocation:
you, the Father, from eternity have thought of us,
wanted us and loved us;
you, the Son, chose us and called us
to share in your unique
and eternal priesthood:
you, the Holy Spirit, have filled us with your gifts
and consecrated us with your holy anointing.
You, the Lord of time and of history,
have placed us on the threshold
of the third Christian millennium,
in order to be witnesses to the salvation
that you have accomplished for all humanity.
We, the Church that proclaims your glory,
implore you:
let there never be a shortage of holy priests

to serve the Gospel;
in every cathedral
and in every corner of the world
let the hymn *"Veni Creator Spiritus"*
resound.
Come O Creator Spirit!
Come and raise up
new generations of young people,
ready to work in the vineyard of the Lord,
to spread the Kingdom of God
to the farthest ends of the earth.
And you, Mary, Mother of Christ,
who at the foot of the Cross accepted us
as beloved sons with the Apostle John,
continue to watch over our vocation.
To you we entrust the years of ministry
that Providence
will grant us yet to live.
Be near us to guide us
along the paths of the world,
to meet the men and women
whom your Son redeemed with his blood.
Help us to fulfill completely
the will of Jesus,
born of you for the salvation of humanity.
O Christ, you are our hope!
"In te, Domine, speravi,
non confundar in aeternum."

LETTER TO PRIESTS FOR HOLY THURSDAY,
MARCH 17, 1996

For Peace

May those in authority be persuaded
that war is an adventure with no return!
No more war!
Grant that there may be
peace in our time!

Let us pray for peace and justice

Let us pray for Italy and for Europe. Let us pray for men and families. Let us pray for peoples and for the Church. Let us pray for peace in Europe and all other parts of the world. Let us pray for freedom, which corresponds to the value of the ideas and works of mankind. Let us pray for social justice and for genuine love, without which human life does not breathe deeply. Let us pray for an end to the terrible threat which modern means of destruction carry with them, an end to the threat that is hidden in the hearts of men, ready to kill and destroy.

Let us also pray for the Church, which, amid the trials of the world, seeks unity in Christ. This is her constant conversion, especially in the present moment of repentance and conversion. May the Church turn to Christ, to her Lord and Redeemer, Teacher and Bridegroom.

MARCH 23, 1980

Brotherhood, peace, and love

Let us pray that the world may never again see a day as terrible as that when the bomb was dropped on Hiroshima.

Let us pray that men will never again place their trust, their calculation, their prestige in weapons so unspeakable and so immoral.

Let us pray that all nations will join together and agree to ban the deadly capacity to construct, multiply, and maintain such weapons, which are the terror of all peoples.

Let us pray that that lethal explosion did not, in seeking peace, also kill it; did not wound forever the honor of science; and did not extinguish the serenity of life on earth.

Let us pray that brotherhood, peace, and love may be granted instead and assured to the world. Let us remember that only Christ can guarantee us these supreme gifts: only he, our Savior, who became our Brother, when Mary said, "Let it be," and became the Mother of Christ.

AUGUST 4, 1985

Peace to you!

Peace to you, dear *brothers and sisters,* who at this moment are listening to me here, at the tomb of St. Peter. And to you who, everywhere on the earth, are united with us.

Peace to you: *All churches* of the people of God that in communion with he who presides over charity form a single Church: the Body of Christ, extending throughout the world.

Peace to you all, brothers and sisters, who together with us confess the same Christ even *if you are not in the unity of the same Church with us.* Together we implore the Consoling Spirit that the time of this union may approach, which had its beginning in the event of Pentecost in Jerusalem.

Peace to you all, brothers and sisters, *who are united by the universal priesthood in the Sacrament of Holy Baptism;* and especially you who, taking this priesthood as the foundation, have given yourselves totally to Christ with your religious vows.

Peace to you, presbyters of the Church, servants of God and of the people of God everywhere on the earth.

Peace to you, *venerated brothers in the Episcopate,* servants and pastors of this people.

Peace to you, venerated *College of Cardinals,* today renewed and enriched by new members.

Peace to you, *Church of God!*

Peace to you, *world of today.* May the Spirit of peace live in you, renewing the face of the earth!

MAY 26, 1985

O Lord, help us build a culture without violence

O Lord and God of everything, you willed that all your children, united by the Spirit, should live and grow together in mutual acceptance, in harmony and peace. Our hearts are overflowing with affliction, because our human selfishness and greed have kept your plan from being accomplished in our time.

We recognize that peace is a gift that comes from you. We know, too, that our collaboration as your instruments requires that we manage the resources of the earth wisely, for the true progress of all peoples. It requires a profound respect and veneration for life, a lively regard for human dignity and the sacredness of each person's conscience, and a constant struggle against all forms of discrimination, in law and deed.

Together with all our brothers and sisters, we undertake to develop a deeper awareness of your presence and your action in history, to be more effective in truth and responsibility, and to work untiringly for freedom from all forms of oppression, brotherhood across every barrier, and justice and fullness of life for all.

We invoke your blessing on the leaders of this nation and all nations, on the followers of all religious traditions, and on all men of good will. Enable us, O Lord, to live and grow in active cooperation with you and all others, with the common aim of building a culture without violence, a world community that entrusts its security not to the construction of deadly weapons but to mutual trust and eagerness to work for a better future for all your children, in a *world civilization built of love, truth, and peace.*

FEBRUARY 2, 1986

Workers for peace

We wish to be workers for peace, because we recognize in creation the signs of God's wisdom, and we wish to live in peace, welcoming the gift of creation as a "good thing," as a sign and Sacrament of God's eternal love for all who live on this planet.

We place our hopes in the heart of Mary, the Mother of the Redeemer, relying on her loving care. To her, the Mother of God and our mother, we entrust the contemporary world's expectations of peace, the expectations of a time so full of significant events, so rich in profound changes. To her we entrust our intense desire that justice and love may prevail over all temptations to violence, revenge, corruption. We ask her that the word of the Gospel, the voice of Christ the Redeemer, may reach the hearts of all people through the mission of the Church.

In this period of the life of mankind, when we feel, with increasing evidence, how important are the obligations and the values of solidarity among nations, of consciously working toward an authentic world community, and are aware, too, of the cost, we ask God to help us respond to the gift of reconciliation, and build the hoped-for civilization of love.

We entrust our prayer to the Mother of the Redeemer, who was born in Bethlehem, so that God may turn his face toward us and grant us peace.

JANUARY 1, 1990

For a lasting peace

Brothers and sisters, let us join our voices and pray for peace and harmony in the entire world, so that all the people God loves may work tirelessly to promote justice, which alone can guarantee a true and lasting peace.

O God, Creator of the universe, who extend to every creature your paternal care and guide the events of history toward the goal of salvation, we recognize your Fatherly love when you soften man's hardness, and open a world torn by conflict and strife to reconciliation. Renew for us the miracles of your mercy: send your Spirit to act in the depths of our hearts, so that enemies may be ready for dialogue, adversaries shake hands, and peoples come together in harmony. Help us commit ourselves to search sincerely for true peace that ends disputes, for charity that conquers hatred, for forgiveness that stifles revenge.

Through Christ our Lord.

Amen.

MARCH 6, 1991

Give us peace!

With living faith we continue to invoke the Lord, may he banish the danger that hangs over us, and may our entreaty, with that of all Christians, become a unanimous cry asking for the great gift of peace.

I am sure that the voices of many believers in God join in this invocation, for they, too, are convinced that the supreme goods of peace and justice can and must coexist, because they correspond to the most profound needs of individuals and peoples.

Lord, hear us!

To you, Mary, Queen of Peace, we entrust, faithfully, our anxiety and our prayer: let men set out on the road of peace confidently and decisively!

It is the only valid way to insure that justice triumphs today!

It is the only road worthy of civilization!

O Lord, give us peace!

JANUARY 13, 1991

No more war!

God of our Fathers,
great and merciful,
Lord of peace and of life,
Father of all.

Your plan is for peace and not for suffering,
you condemn war
and you humble the pride of the aggressor.

You sent your son Jesus
to proclaim peace near and far,
to unite men
of every race and every ethnicity
in a single family.

Hear the unanimous cry of your children,
the heartfelt supplication of all humanity:
no more war, an adventure without return,
no more war,
a spiral of grief and violence.

In communion with Mary, the Mother of Jesus,
we pray to you again:
speak to the hearts of those who decide
the destinies of peoples,
stop the cycle of retaliation
and revenge,

suggest with your Spirit new solutions,
generous and honorable gestures,
periods of dialogue and patient waiting
more fruitful than the swift actions
of war.

Grant in our time days of peace.
No more war.
Amen.

JANUARY 16, 1991

Let us pray for peace

Brothers and sisters,

Anxiety and distress, which, unfortunately, have been expressed many times already over the war going on in the Gulf region, continue to be nourished by the persistent conflicts, and now, in addition, there are also catastrophic environmental risks.

The victims, both civilian and military, and the enormous destruction intensify our grief, and we are all called upon to address the Lord more insistently and with a stronger faith: it is the great recourse available to those who believe and have hope in divine mercy.

Let us pray above all for peace: that God may grant it as soon as possible, enlightening our leaders so that they may quickly abandon that road which is unworthy of humanity, and seek justice confidently through dialogue and negotiation! May the efforts of those who, generously, continue to propose initiatives to stop the conflict be crowned with success.

Let us pray for the civilian populations that are enduring bombardments or have been forced, in the hundreds of thousands, to abandon their homes and their native land, and to face the tragic experience of refugees: may God grant them comfort and inspire in all people feelings and initiatives of real solidarity!

Let us pray that the tragedy that is taking place does not become more brutal and inhuman through actions unacceptable in terms of both ethical values and international treaties. The news that has reached us concerning the fate of prisoners of war and the threat of recourse to the weapons of terrorism is a particular cause of anguish.

May God remove the temptation to use such means, which are contrary to the most elementary moral principles and condemned by international law!

Let us pray again for and with all believers belonging to the three religions that have their historical roots in the Middle East: Jews, Christians, and Muslims. Faith in the same God must be a cause not of conflict and rivalry but of a commitment to overcome differences through dialogue and negotiations.

May the infinite love of the Creator help all to understand the absurdity of a war in his name and instill in every heart true feelings of trust, understanding, and cooperation for the good of all humanity!

We faithfully entrust these aims to the Most Holy Virgin, Queen of Peace.

JANUARY 27, 1991

May the peace given by your Son flourish

God of our Fathers,
Father of all,
who in your Son Jesus, the Prince of Peace,
proclaimed peace near and far,
to unite men
of every race and every creed
in a single family,
we implore you to grant
life without end and your peace
to the dead on all fronts,
who, many unidentified, lie
in this earth, which is bathed in their blood.
May their sacrifice and their heroism—
while opening hearts to gratitude
and reviving the great ideals of freedom
and love on mother earth—
arouse the desire for tolerance,
nonviolence, and peace.
For this reason, in communion with Mary,
the Mother of Jesus,
we pray, O Father,
that all those who climb
the steps of this memorial chapel
may be enlightened by the Spirit of your Son
and develop in their hearts
the desire to work for peace,

for all creatures.
Enlighten the leaders of nations,
so that, in view of the lesson
that history demonstrates,
they will no longer entrust to war the job
of resolving the problems
of living together among peoples.
May the peace given by your Son,
crucified and risen,
flourish in our lands,
and bring to men and women
in our time
a taste for developing those values
which build up your Kingdom
and never fade.
Amen.

May 3, 1992

For the Family

The future of mankind
passes by way of the family!
It is therefore indispensable and urgent
that every person of good will
endeavor to save and foster
the values and requirements of the family.

Familiaris Consortio
(Apostolic Exhortation,
November 22, 1981)

Prayer for the Synod on the family

God, who are the Father of everything in Heaven and on earth, Father, who are love and life, make every human family on the earth become, through your Son Jesus Christ, "born of woman," and through the Holy Spirit, the source of divine charity, a true sanctuary of life and love for the generations to come. May your grace direct the thoughts and deeds of spouses to the good of their families and all the families of the world. May the younger generations find in the family strong support for their humanity, so that they may grow in truth and love. May love, strengthened by the grace of the Sacrament of Matrimony, prove to be stronger than any weakness or crisis that, at any time, our families must endure. Finally we ask you that the Church, through the intercession of the Holy Family of Nazareth, may successfully complete among all the nations of the earth her mission in the family through the family. You, who are life, the truth, and love, in the unity of the Son and the Holy Spirit. Amen.

AUGUST 15, 1980

Loving the family means being able to appreciate its values and capabilities, fostering them always.

Loving the family means identifying the dangers and evils that menace it, in order to overcome them.

Loving the family means endeavoring to create an environment favorable for its development. The modern Christian family is often tempted to be discouraged and is distressed by its increasing difficulties; it is an eminent form of love to give it back its reasons for confidence in itself, in the riches it possesses by nature and grace, in the mission that God has entrusted to it.

The families of today
must be called back to
their original position!
They must follow Christ!

Familiaris Consortio

Confidence in families

May St. Joseph, "the just man," a tireless worker, the upright guardian of those entrusted to his care, guard, protect, and enlighten families forever.

May the Virgin Mary, who is the Mother of the Church, thus also be the Mother of the "Church of the home." Thanks to her motherly aid, may every Christian family truly become a "little church," in which the mystery of the Church of Christ is mirrored and given new life. May she, the Handmaiden of the Lord, be an example of humble and generous acceptance of the will of God; may she, the sorrowful Mother at the foot of the Cross, comfort the sufferings and dry the tears of those who are in distress because of the difficulties in their families.

And may Christ the Lord, the Universal King, the King of families, be present in every Christian home as he was at Cana, bestowing light, joy, serenity and strength. On the solemn day dedicated to his Kingship I beg of him that every family may generously make its own contribution to the coming of his Kingdom in the world—"a Kingdom of Truth and Life, a Kingdom of Holiness and Grace, a Kingdom of justice, love, and peace," toward which history is journeying.

I entrust each family to him, to Mary, to Joseph. To their hands and their hearts I offer this Exhortation: may it be they who present it to you, venerable brothers and beloved sons and daughters, and who open your hearts to the light that the Gospel sheds on every family.

Familiaris Consortio

In prayer for the family

We offer special thanks at this time for the Christian families of our parish.

Together with his son Jesus Christ our Lord, we thank the Father "from whom every family takes its name."

We thank him:

–For all the many families of the parish whose life reflects "the beauty and grandeur of the vocation to love and the service of life";

Lord, bless our families.

–For the deep love that Christian spouses exchange in the communion of marital life, keeping alive in the world an utterly special image of the love of God;

Lord, bless our families.

–For the life of mutual faith lived by innumerable couples, thanks to the power of Sacramental Grace;

Lord, bless our families.

–For all those couples who strive generously to follow God's plan of human love, which is expressed by the teaching of the Church in *Humanae Vitae* and *Familiaris Consortio,* and whose marriage is always open to new life; and for all those who help educate couples in natural family planning;

Lord, bless our families.

–For the great, extraordinary service rendered by parents in bringing new members to the mystical body of Christ;

Lord, bless our families.

–For the continuing involvement of fathers and mothers

in the education of their children to Christian maturity;

Lord, bless our families.

—For families who despite suffering, pain, and economic hardship live a life of Christian hope;

Lord, bless our families.

—For the commitment of families, in conformity with the teaching of the Second Vatican Council, to participate actively in the mission of the Church, as a community of believers and evangelizers and as a community in dialogue with God and in the service of man;

Lord, bless our families.

—For the efforts of Christian families to help young people understand the dignity of marriage and prepare themselves adequately for this vocation;

Lord, bless our families.

—For the renewed commitment of the Church to support and teach the holiness and the unity of the family, and for the generous love with which so many priests and religious dedicate their energies to building family life;

Lord, bless our families.

—For the efforts of those families that have encountered problems and difficulties but have persevered in the conviction that the eternal and indestructible love of God for man is expressed in the indissoluble bond of their sacramental marriage;

Lord, bless our families.

—For the special testimony to Christ's teaching on the indissolubility of marriage given by all spouses who suffer the pain of separation, abandonment, or rejection;

Lord, bless our families.

–For spreading the message of the Gospel among Christian families, and for the evangelization that is carried out by families among their neighbors and in their workplace;

Lord, bless our families.

–For the many families that pray together and draw strength from the worship of God;

Lord, bless our families.

–For the families that embrace the Cross and share in the Christian joy of the Paschal Mystery of the Lord Jesus;

Lord, bless our families.
We give thanks to you and praise you,
God our Father,
for all the Christian families
who listen to the words of life
of Jesus Christ your Son:
"Let your light so shine
before men,
that they may see your good works
and give glory to your Father
who is in Heaven."
May we, together with all the families
of our parish,
respond to the Christian vocation,
each of us according to the gifts we have received,
each through the witness
of our good works.
May each of us

hear the call
to give glory to you,
Lord our God.
Through Christ our Lord.
Amen.

SEPTEMBER 12, 1984

Building up the family with prayer

Let us pray as a *great community of families,* which desire to give testimony of their vocation in Christ.

He himself said: "For where two or three are gathered in my name, there am I in the midst of them."

Through prayer uttered in the community of the family we invite Christ to be among us: spouses, parents, and children.

Prayer is the first testimony of our vocation. We give that testimony to Christ one after another. With that testimony *we become witnesses reciprocally.*

Through prayer we build the family, which is the domestic Church.

Let us pray today for the unity in our families that comes from prayer.

Let us pray that Christian families may pray, and pray without reserve. It is the first condition for carrying out the tasks that Christ and the Church place before them.

"The Angel of the Lord brought the announcement to Mary, and she conceived through the action of the Holy Spirit." Joseph, instructed from on high, was not afraid to take her with him.

She conceived, she carried Jesus Christ in her womb and gave him to the world: the Eternal Word, made flesh.

The Son of God, for the salvation of the world. He accepted *the human family of Nazareth* as his own and made it holy. For most of his life on earth he lived in that family. In this way he is united, in a certain sense, *with every human family* and on every one he has stamped the sign of holiness.

The family was the hiding place of the Son of God on earth. There he led his hidden life. But in it also he hid the treasures of life and holiness.

May we, through the work of the Synod of Bishops, be able to reveal Christ more fully to every human family.

May we, thanks to the daily common prayer of families all over the world, *succeed in reaching the riches* that the Son of God hid in the family, having lived in it for some thirty years.

During one of the sessions of the Synod, Mother Teresa of Calcutta spoke thus to the gathered bishops: Give us holy priests! Send us holy priests as servants of Christ and as dispensers of the mysteries of God.

And where will those priests come from, if not from families that live the spirit of Christ?

Oh! On this day, inspire in all the bishops and priests of the Church a great love for families!

Encourage, reinforce, and deepen the pastoral work of families throughout the world. May families, with the help of their pastors, find the roads that lead to the fulfillment of their duties in the contemporary world.

And may all the Christian families in the entire world pray for priests, *may they pray for priestly and religious vocations,* may they become the "domestic church," the primary seedbed of vocations.

The harvest is plentiful!

OCTOBER 12, 1980

God's collaborators

Dear brothers and sisters!

God has deigned to choose man and woman to collaborate, with love and labor, in his work of creation and redemption of the world.

Together let us raise a prayer to God, appealing to the intercession of St. Joseph, the head of the Holy Family of Nazareth and Patron of the universal Church.

Let us pray together and say: *Hear us, O Lord!*

For all the pastors and ministers of the Church, that they may serve the people of God with energetic and generous dedication, as St. Joseph worthily served the Lord Jesus and the Virgin Mother, let us pray.

For leaders of governments, so that, in serving the common good, they may order economic and social life with justice and rectitude, with respect for the law and the dignity of all, let us pray.

That God may consent to join to the passion of his Son the labors and sufferings of workers, the anxiety of the unemployed, and the pain of the oppressed, and that he may give help and comfort to all, let us pray.

For all our families and for all their members: parents, children, old people, so that, with respect for the life and personality of each, they may contribute to the growth of faith and charity, to be authentic witnesses of the Gospel, let us pray.

O Lord,
give to your faithful
the Spirit of truth and peace,
so that they may know you with their entire soul,
and, as they generously do
what is pleasing to you,
may always enjoy your blessings.
For Christ our Lord.
Amen.

March 19, 1980

Prayer to the Holy Family

O Holy Family of Nazareth,
the community of love
of Jesus, Mary, and Joseph,
the model and ideal of every Christian family,
to you we entrust our families.

Open the heart of every home
to faith, to acceptance of the Word of God
to Christian witness,
so that it may become the source
of new and holy vocations.

Prepare the minds of parents,
so that, with urgent charity,
wise care, and loving piety,
they may guide their children surely
in the direction of spiritual and eternal goods.

Inspire in the souls of the young
an upright conscience and a free will,
so that, growing in "wisdom,
age, and grace,"
they may generously accept
the gift of the divine vocation.

O Holy Family of Nazareth,
make us all available to carry out the will of God,

by contemplating and imitating
the assiduous prayer,
the generous obedience,
the dignified poverty,
and the virginal purity lived in you,
and to accompany with prudent delicacy
those among us who are called
to follow more nearly the Lord Jesus,
who "gave himself" for us.
Amen.

1994

O Holy Family

be a guide for families everywhere on earth!
Family, Holy Family, may your example guide us and protect us!

Family, Holy Family—the Family so closely united to the mystery that we contemplate on the day of the Lord's birth, may your example guide families everywhere on earth!

Son of God, who came among us in the warmth of a family, grant that all families may grow in love and contribute to the good of mankind through a commitment to faithful and fruitful unity, respect for life, and a striving for brotherly solidarity with all.

Teach them, therefore, to put aside selfishness, lying, and unrestrained greed.

Help them to develop the immense resources of their hearts and minds, which multiply when it is you who inspire them.

Baby Jesus, dry
the tears of children!
Caress the old and the sick!

Urge men to lay down their weapons and hold each other in a universal embrace.

Invite all peoples, merciful Jesus, to tear down the walls created by misery and by unemployment, by ignorance and indifference, by discrimination and intolerance.

It is you, divine Child of Bethlehem, who save us, delivering us from sin.

It is you who are the true and only Savior, toward whom humanity gropes its way.

God of peace, gift of peace for all humanity, come and dwell in the heart of every man and every family.

Be our peace and our joy!

DECEMBER 25, 1994

Believe and You Will Live

The primary basis of work
is man himself, who is its subject . . .
in the first place
work is "for man,"
and not man "for work."

LABOREM EXERCENS
(ENCYCLICAL,
SEPTEMBER 14, 1981)

Hasten, people

Christians of every continent,
committed to the difficult but necessary
road of unity and peace, and you, men of good will
who listen to me,
let us hasten, pilgrims all,
to the manger of Bethlehem.
Into the stable, where Jesus
speaks of innocence and peace,
we enter to listen to
a fundamental lesson.
Hasten, O humanity, scattered and fearful,
to beg for peace, a gift and task
for every individual of noble and generous feeling.
Enough of hatred and tyranny!
No more war.
No more indifference and silence
toward those who ask for understanding and solidarity,
toward the laments of those who are
dying of hunger,
among the waste and abundance of goods.
How can we forget those who suffer,
who are alone or abandoned, depressed and discouraged,
who have neither home nor job,
who are victims of oppression and abuse,
and of the many forms of
modern totalitarianism?
How can we allow economic interests

to reduce the human person
to an instrument of profit,
allow creatures not yet born
to be killed,
innocent children
to be humiliated and taken advantage of,
the old and the sick
to be outcast and abandoned?
Only you, Word Incarnate, born of Mary,
can make us brothers and sisters,
children in the Child,
children in the semblance of the Child.
Future glory was revealed to us
through you, the Son of Mary,
the Son of Man,
whence we can cry out: "Abba, Father!"
through you . . .
Amen!

DECEMBER 25, 1991

Walk

"In the name of Jesus Christ of Nazareth, walk!"

Walk!

Walk, young people, in the name of Jesus Christ, without fear of hardships and obstacles: be the herald of new hope, which flows from the mystery of his Cross. In him we have overcome the world.

Walk in trust, cleaning out "the old leaven, to be a new dough": in the family, whose fundamental value, owing to the rapid changes taking place in the world today, is experiencing a profound crisis; in the schools, in the workplace, in the parish, and in all other areas of society.

Be aware that you are not alone on this path: Mary, the Mother of the Redeemer, stands guard by your side, she who became the Mother of humanity at the foot of the Cross.

May the Saints, who had the courage to give up everything, even life, to preserve their faith, be an example to you. May their aid, and their heavenly intercession, obtain for each of you the indispensable strength of spirit to enable you to fearlessly bear witness to a firm adherence to Christ and his Church.

I, too, walk with you, I follow you and encourage you with prayer, and I bless all who are good-hearted.

MAY 3, 1992

Young people, believe and you will live!

Because you exist, there is someone who has reserved something great for you. Listen to me, for I am about to announce it! Just as the Apostles Peter and John said to the man who, dressed in rags and lame from birth, was begging at the entrance to the Temple in Jerusalem, the Pope says to you: *"I have no silver or gold, but I give you what I have: in the name of Jesus Christ of Nazareth, walk!"* Yes, young friends, the Pope has come here today to *give you the strength of Christ, to give you a companion you may have confidence in!*

Can you have confidence, even just once, in someone who has never disappointed anyone? Open your heart to Jesus Christ and you will know the courage that never fails, however great the obstacles: you will know a love stronger than death! In the presence of this multitude of young people, I cannot help bearing witness to this power of God, praising this sure love that has already saved my life from death!

Young people, believe and you will live!
Young people, believe
and bet everything on love!
Young people,
believe and decide this very day
to build in your life a structure for eternity! My young friends and brothers, find again the faith in yourselves and build your lives, your love, your families in Christ! Because: *"I am sure that neither death, nor life, nor angels, nor principalities, nor*

things present, nor things to come, nor powers, nor height, nor depth, nor anything else in all creation, will be able to separate us from the love of God in Christ Jesus our Lord." A young person faithful to Christ will know true happiness that has no end.

JUNE 7, 1992

Man of our time!

Man, you who live immersed in the world,
believing that you are its master
when perhaps you are its prey,
Christ will free you from every bond
to launch you in the conquest of yourself,
in constructive love, extended to the good;
exacting love,
that makes you the builder, not the destroyer,
of your tomorrow, of your family,
of your environment, of the whole of society.
Man of our time!
Only Christ Resurrected
can satisfy fully
your unsuppressible aspiration to freedom.
After the atrocities of two world wars
and all the wars that,
in these fifty years,
often in the name of atheist ideologies,
have mowed down victims
and sowed hatred in so many nations;
after years of dictatorships
that have deprived man
of his fundamental freedoms,
the true dimensions of the spirit
have been rediscovered,
those which the Church has always promoted,
revealing in Christ the true stature of man.

Also, the awakening of many democracies
leads today to dialogue
and trust among peoples;
and the world understands again
that man cannot live without God!
Without the Truth that, in him, makes man free.
Man of our time!
Christ frees you from selfishness
and calls you to share,
and to a swift and joyous
commitment to others.
Man of today!
Wealthy nations of an opulent civilization!
Do not be indifferent to the world's many tragedies,
be increasingly aware of the need
to help those peoples
who struggle every day
for survival.
Believe that there is no freedom
where misery persists.
May human and Christian solidarity be
the challenge that stimulates your conscience
so that the sand
may yield a little at a time
to the promotion of human dignity,
and make the bread take shape
to give back a smile, work,
hope, progress.
But, thanks to God, I have also seen
single people, associations, institutions,

priests, religious, lay people in various professions
voluntarily commit themselves and sacrifice themselves
for the good of their lonely and suffering brothers and
sisters.
I thank them in the name of Christ crucified and
risen!
Man of our time!
Christ *frees you because he loves you,*
because he gave himself for you
because he overcame for you and for all men.
Christ restored the world and you to God.
He restored God to you and to the world.
For ever!
"Be of good cheer, I have overcome the world!"
With this complete confidence
in Christ's love
for man who lives, hopes, suffers,
and loves in every latitude
of the globe,
I greet the various peoples and nations,
in their own languages,
and wish for all of you the joy and
the peace of the Risen Christ.

APRIL 15, 1990

Do not forget the Creator

To you, humanity, who look with pleasure on the works of your hand, the fruit of your genius, Christ says to you: Do not forget the One who gave birth to all! Do not forget the Creator! Further, the more profoundly you know the laws of nature, the more you discover its wealth and potential, the more intensely you must remember him.

Do not forget the Creator—Christ tells us—and respect Creation! Do your work using the resources that God has given you as they should be used! Transform these riches with the help of science and technology, but do not abuse them; be neither a usurper nor an exploiter, without considering the goods that have been created! Do not destroy or contaminate! Remember your neighbor, and the poor! Think of the future generations!

MAY 10, 1990

Special thanks to Rick Garson, chairman of Compulsion Entertainment. Thanks also to the Libreria Editrice Rogate (LER), Father Nunzio Spinelli, and the Very Reverend Father Leonardo Sapienza, respectively, for the publication and the compilation of the anthologies. And to Alan R. Kershaw, Advocate of the Apostolic Tribunal of the Roman Rota, Paul Schnidler, Esq., Larry Shire, Esq., Gil Karson, Esq., of Grubman, Indusrky and Schindler. Also to Michael Abramson, Tenisha Ramos, Michael Mitchell, Jim Gallina, and Enzo Zullo for making this a global message.

KAROL WOJTYLA, POPE JOHN PAUL II, was born in Wadowice in Poland, in 1920. He studied literature and drama in Krakow and later worked at a stone quarry and at a chemical plant. During the German occupation of Poland in World War II he began preparing for the priesthood and was ordained in 1946. Wojtyla became bishop of Krakow in 1958, archbishop in 1964, and cardinal in 1967. He was elected Pope in 1978 and is the 264th bishop of Rome.